SUPERDUTCH
NEW
ARCHITECTURE
IN THE
NETHERLANDS

BART
LOOTSMA

Thames & Hudson

Special photography by Christian Richters

First published in the United Kingdom in 2000 by Thames & Hudson Ltd, 181A High Holborn, London WC1V 7QX

British Library Cataloguing-in-Publication Data
A catalogue record for this book is available from the British Library

ISBN 0-500-34178-8

Designed by Mevis en van Deursen, Amsterdam
Printed and bound in Singapore by Tien Wah Press

This publication was made possible with the support of the Netherlands Architecture Fund.

PHOTOGRAPHY CREDITS

Unless noted below, photographs were taken by Christian Richters.

Aeroview: 59
Michel Boesveld: 220–29
Jan Derwig: 50–52
Droog Design: 18
Glenn Halvorson: 99, 100–01
Atelier van Lieshout: 88–91, 97
Luchtfoto: 10
Carry Markerink: 93
Max 1:
Jeroen Musch:
NL Architects: 253
Kas Oosterhuis:
Bas Princen: 2, 7, 255–57
Peter de Ruig: 230–31
West 8: 22
Hans Werlemann: 139–40, 197–202, 204–07, 247, 252 (top)
Dirk Jan Woudstra: 86–87, 94–96, 99
Kim Zwarts: 26–49, 54–56, 203

THE SECOND MODERNITY OF DUTCH ARCHITECTURE

During the 1990s it became apparent that something special was happening in Dutch architecture. It began with Rem Koolhaas, who advanced a series of innovative designs and theories that represented a radical break with the prevailing wisdom about architecture while struggling to achieve an entirely new basis for it. Koolhaas had in fact been preoccupied with these aims since the mid-1970s, but as the 1980s progressed his work grew stronger and his ideas found recognition among an expanding international circle of people.

The interest aroused by Koolhaas and his practice Office of Metropolitan Architecture (OMA), prompted magazines, museums and educational institutions to seek other interesting architecture being produced in the Netherlands, and it soon became clear that there were many examples of innovation. Besides the designs themselves, the comparative youthfulness of many of these designers began to draw attention from abroad. Many of them had erected their first projects during the 1980s, when they were not yet thirty, and in some cases before they had even finished their training. Practices like those of Wiel Arets, Ben van Berkel and, a little later, West 8, MVRDV, Neutelings and NOX, were turning out one striking plan after another. Compared to other countries, moreover, a relatively large proportion of these designs were actually being built. These architects followed Rem Koolhaas's example with provocative lectures, books and exhibitions. Like him, too, they took positions of influence as visiting or permanent professors at such elite international architecture schools as the Architectural Association in London, Columbia University in New York and Harvard University in Boston.

The reason that there have been so many interesting developments in Dutch architecture during the past ten years is not just a sudden outbreak of talent. There is no reason to suppose that the capabilities of young architects in the Netherlands have been any greater than those elsewhere during the same period, but their collective talent enjoyed unquestionably better opportunities. To some extent the encouragement offered to young architects is a sound Dutch tradition. The cream of the generation of architects currently in their sixties, such as Carel Weeber, Cees Dam, Wim Quist and Herman Hertzberger, also realized their first projects before they were thirty. But youthfulness is no more than a very general sign of innovation and talent. Rem Koolhaas, for instance, did not erect his first building until 1984, when he was forty.

To understand this surge of activity, it is helpful to consider the period from a broader perspective. In 1989 a number of radical changes began to affect Dutch society, and thus the context in which architecture was evolving. The most significant of these was undoubtedly the internationalization that played a part in every aspect of society and culture. Although internationalization had been an active force in Dutch society for some time, it was in 1989 – significantly the same year that the Berlin Wall fell – when it began to gain noticeable momentum. The culture of any country opening up to internationalization is generally subject to two opposing forces: on the one hand, there is a reassessment (critical or otherwise) of the practical value of national traditions, and on the other a wish to participate in the main international developments – to make the national voice heard within them. Both tendencies are evident in the Dutch architecture of recent decades. The strength of Dutch architecture during the 1990s is that it succeeded in finding a place within an international architectural discourse without sacrificing the typically Dutch qualities of realism and *Sachlichkeit* (matter-of-factness).

GROWTH

The Netherlands has experienced a period of tremendous population growth during the twentieth century. Stichting Wonen, a foundation whose task was to study housing issues and which merged with several other foundations in 1990 to form the newly established Netherlands Architecture Institute (NAI) in Rotterdam, calculated in 1986 that over 70 per cent of the built environment in the Netherlands had been created since World War II. By the year 2000 that figure had reached over 75

Oosterlijk Flevoland

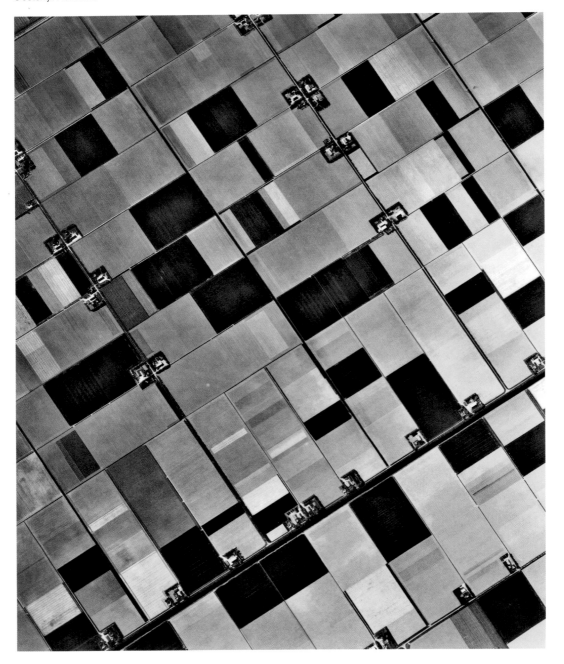

per cent. The population density of the Benelux countries – Belgium, the Netherlands and Luxembourg – is as a whole similar to that of Japan; the population density of the Netherlands alone is even higher than Japan's. The country's strategic location around the combined deltas of the Rhine, Mense and Schelde rivers has clearly been a contributing factor to this growth. The harbour of Rotterdam expanded during the twentieth century to become the biggest in the world, and the Netherlands has worked hard to retain its status as the 'main port' of Europe and to consolidate and expand its reputation in air transportation. Schiphol Airport will be developed extensively in coming years, and the country's rail links with Europe's interior are to be enhanced for both goods and high-speed passenger traffic.

THE FIRST MODERNITY

A large area of the country lies below sea level and thus throughout much of its modern history has had to be protected from flooding by artificial means. A significant portion of the existing land area has been reclaimed from the sea, while other areas have either subsided as the result of centuries of continuous mechanical drainage or fallen below the rising average sea level due to climatic change. Such factors determine the appearance of the landscape, the way land is used, the way people deal with the built environment, and the appearance of buildings. Unspoilt countryside does not exist in the Netherlands, except perhaps the Wadden Sea area. Even the country's many nature reserves have been planned and designed, land 'returned to nature' and paradoxically cultivated as part of an intensive conservation programme.

The Dutch landscape is largely new – indeed, very new. Drainage of the former Zuider Zee became legally and financially possible in 1918 while World War I was still in progress. The first polder, or stretch of reclaimed land, to emerge from the waters of the Zuider Zee, Wieringermeer, dates from 1930; the Afsluitdijk, the dyke that turned the Zuider Zee from a sea into a lake called IJsselmeer, was completed only in 1932. The largest polders, Noordoostpolder (drained in 1942) and Flevoland, were not ready for occupation until after World War II. One significant development in this period was the substantial increase in the size of a typical farm field, due to new agricultural technology. The Delta Act, which mandated countless dyke constructions and reinforcement programmes, as well as the famous tidal barrier and other hydrological works on the Zeeland coast, was passed in 1953, just after floods had inundated a large part of the Dutch province of Zeeland. A 1954 act of parliament enabled the mass redrawing of field boundaries across large areas in order make farming more efficient, thereby changing the pattern of agricultural land and its use in much of the country. In the 1950s and 1960s the government funded large-scale development projects to cope with the housing shortage caused by the effects of wartime destruction, the stagnation of building production and maintenance, and, above all, the demand for new houses engendered by the post-war baby boom. The innovative mass-production building methods that were subsidized for this demand had an effect on the character and mentality of Dutch construction companies that persists to this day. Another post-war phenomenon affecting the land has been the staggering growth in personal mobility that has overwhelmed the landscape with new motorways, railways and large-scale transport engineering works, thereby feeding the many new areas of housing and industry.

To sum up, the Netherlands has a tradition of dealing with the built environment by a level-headed and pragmatic application of technology and planning. There is also a significant tradition of consultation, historically necessary because the need for careful water management obliged affected landowners to collaborate closely in what were known as 'water boards', which formed an important organ of government in parallel with municipal and provincial administrations.

STAGNATION

Most of these land developments took place in the unusually optimistic atmosphere of the post-war reconstruction period. People cherished ambitions that went far beyond merely recovering from the consequences of the war and the occupation. An idea grew that it must be possible to reconstruct the whole of society and so dispense with poverty and inequality. Collective self-discipline and solidarity resulted in a substantial rise in general welfare and the construction of an elaborate system of social measures. Indeed, the Netherlands grew into a prime example of a Western welfare state.

By the early 1960s, however, disappointment about the lack of genuine social and cultural change and a longing for increased consultation and mental liberation struck the first blows at the political atmosphere and mechanisms that had encouraged the dynamic post-war reconstruction of the Netherlands. Further pressure was applied by the oil crisis of 1973 and the report of the Club of Rome, which made people aware that there might well be limits to growth, or that if there were not, such limits should be set. The architectural community was shocked to realize that after years dominated by new large-scale suburban development, the old city-centre districts had fallen into disrepair, and in some cases had been destroyed completely. The new mood was evident in popular protests against such projects as the construction of an underground railway, or against the combined new opera house and city hall (nicknamed the 'Stopera') in Amsterdam. Developments that required the demolition of large areas of the city brought the problem of urban renewal back into the limelight. Architecture as a design discipline was scarcely playing any part in projects at this time. There was a new focus on consultation, as it was felt that the original inhabitants of the affected areas were entitled to have a say about how the renovation should take place. The changed climate also had wider consequences for the landscape and urban planning, which have persisted to the present day. Protest movements against the building of housing projects and roads in nature reserves have become common, and as a result elaborate consultation procedures have come into existence, considerably delaying the start of such projects as the

extension of the Rotterdam docks, the expansion of Schiphol Airport, and more generally the building of new motorways and high-speed railway lines. Plans to create a new polder, Markerwaard, have been frozen even though a large section of the dyke has already been built. Areas of the most recently drained polder, South Flevoland, have been 'returned to nature' and are now classed as nature reserves. New residential architecture was consciously designed to be small scale in character, with an emphasis on the individual house, even if it formed part of a larger development. Designs drew freely on historical models despite the same industrial building production methods being used. This led to an almost unnoticed proliferation of deliberately chaotic neighbourhoods and to complete new towns, such as Almere, a place that seems to deny its own urbanity. In cities like Rotterdam, Tilburg and Eindhoven, where large areas had already been demolished in anticipation of massive redevelopment, plans were abandoned and the empty areas filled in with fine-meshed housing. In the municipal government of the larger cities, it proved easier to install local district councils than to establish administrative bodies at the metropolitan level, the so-called 'city provinces' needed for large projects like the Rotterdam docks extension. Thus the first phase of modernity in the Netherlands shuddered to a halt by the end of the 1980s. The Dutch belief in a 'makeable society' vanished, to be replaced by a feeling that the country ought to align itself more closely to international standards and values, also in relation to architecture and urban planning.

THE ROLE OF CULTURAL INSTITUTIONS
By the late 1970s it was clear that architecture was haemorrhaging as a result of the national emphasis on urban renewal. The architectural department of the Rotterdam Arts Council was the first organization to take action. Its primary objective was to shake the Dutch architectural profession out of its isolation by confronting it with trend-setting architects and critics from abroad. They began by inviting such international critics as Stanislaus von Moos and Francesco dal Co to give talks about the city

of Rotterdam. Not long afterwards, in 1982, the Arts Council organized the first Architecture International of Rotterdam (AIR), in which non-Dutch architects J. P. Kleihues, O. M. Ungers, Derek Walker and Aldo Rossi, among others, were invited to prepare sketch designs for Kop van Zuid, a redevelopment zone on the left bank of the Mense in the heart of Rotterdam. Although the area still accommodated various harbour activities, it was clear that these would have to find a new location within the foreseeable future because of the port's continuing expansion. None of the first AIR designs were executed, but they played a visible and significant part in the eventual plan for Kop van Zuid, which has almost been completed. Aside from the development, however, an ideal opportunity had been presented for the people and architects of Rotterdam to make acquaintance with the ideas of the invited designers and to see what implications they might have in a specifically Dutch situation. The first AIR manifestation was followed by Japan-AIR and Iberia-AIR, in which exhibitions and seminars introduced the Netherlands to architects from Japan and Spain respectively. These were followed by a number of AIR forums in which the Rotterdam Arts Council looked ahead to problems that were perceptible in the city even though they were not yet subject to official attention. AIR 1998, titled 'The City as a Stage', concentrated on public space, and AIR-Alexander of 1993 dealt with the treatment of the outermost margins of the city and with the renovation of a 1960s urban extension.

The AIR conferences were outstandingly successful because they created an opportunity to discuss concrete problems at a high level while generating possible design solutions. Although not conceived with immediate implementation in mind, the latter stimulated broad debate among all the parties involved in the building process, ranging from property developers and architects to the general public and politicians. The AIR conferences were imitated in many different forms in other cities, though generally on a smaller scale. Architects such as Rem Koolhaas, Wiel Arets, Adriaan Geuze, Winy Maas, and Jacob van Rijs (the last two now together as MVRDV, although at the time they both worked for OMA), participated in one or more of these events, in which they often entered into debates with foreign architectural celebrities.

The introduction of and dialogue with foreign architects became a common practice in Dutch cities during the 1980s. The trend started with the universities who organized several major symposiums in the late seventies and early eighties, but it was not long before Dutch architectural journals and architectural practices followed suit. Aldo Rossi, Richard Meier, Michael Graves, Alvaro Siza, Coop Himmelb(l)au, Ricardo Bofill, Steven Holl, Charles Vandenhove, Giorgio Grassi, Bernard Tschumi, Daniel Libeskind, Rob Krier, Renzo Piano, Kisho Kurokawa, Norman Foster, Helmut Jahn, Peter Eisenman and many others – astonished to find themselves together – built projects of all sizes. First and foremost it was ambitious Dutch Labour Party members on the councils of The Hague, Groningen and Maastricht who invited foreign architects to the Netherlands. Understandably, this put the noses of local architects out of joint, but the idea was to challenge them to produce the same quality as the visitors. In the 1980s, it was primarily the younger architects who picked up the gauntlet. Among them, Jo Coenen, Sjoerd Soeters and Rudy Uytenhaak aligned themselves with international postmodernism and Benthem Crouwel with High Tech. Practices like Mecanoo and Karelse Van der Meer profited by acting as local architects for such international figures as Alvaro Siza and Bernard Tschumi. Today, Dutch architects and planners are proud of attracting reputable foreign colleagues into their projects.

The greater interest in architecture by the public and politicians that began in the 1980s reached new levels in the following decade. In 1990 the ministries of culture and of housing and planning jointly issued a policy paper outlining plans to stimulate the 'cultural component' of architecture. The paper was followed by a second policy paper in which the ministries of agriculture, and transport and public works have also played a part.[1] The ministries reserved a considerable sum for

1. *Ruimte voor Architectuur, nota voor architectuurbeleid,* Dutch Government (Lower House),1990–, 21 363, nos. 2–3; *De Architectuur van de Ruimte,* Dutch Government (Lower House),1996–.

Marieke Timmermans
New landscape map of the Netherlands

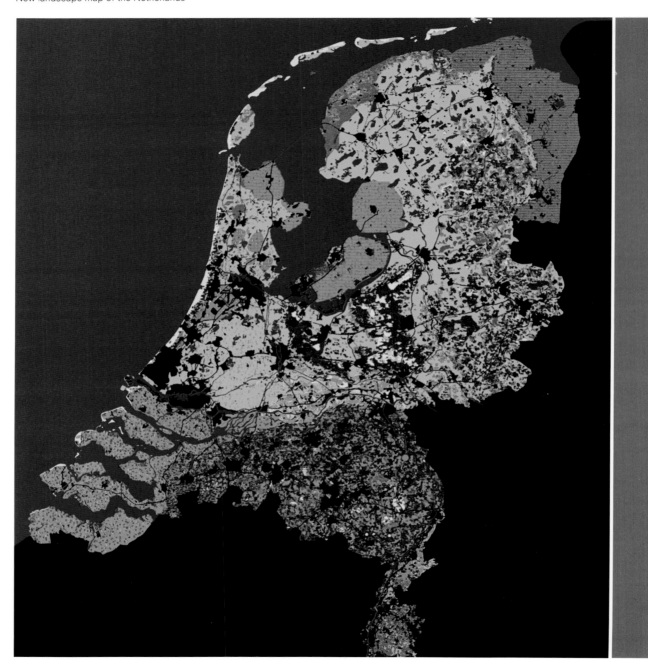

architecture and planning in their budgets and three significant new institutions were established. The Netherlands Architecture Institute, which has been located in Rotterdam since 1989 in recognition of the city's active architectural politics; the Netherlands Architecture Fund, which distributes subsidies for activities organized by third parties, such as events, publications, research and competitions, and promotes the establishment of local architecture centres in larger towns; and the Berlage Institute, established in Amsterdam in 1990, although it moves to Rotterdam in 2000, offers an internationally oriented masters degree course and is intended to compensate for cuts in standard architectural training in the Netherlands.

These new institutions were complemented by an existing subsidy scheme (The Netherlands Foundation for Arts, Design and Architecture), which provides study grants, travel bursaries, exhibition subsidies and similar financial aid to architects within two years of graduation for limited-term special projects external to their normal practice activities. The idea is that architects who have demonstrated a concern for quality in their work will thereby win a stronger competitive position in both the Dutch and international markets. This has become a political matter at a time when the government is relinquishing some of its direct influence on architecture and urban planning. The previous approach of more direct intervention has thus been replaced by a policy of schooling, enticement and debate. But architecture remains political, and it is no coincidence that the first director of the Netherlands Architecture Institute, Adri Duivesteijn, was formerly a city councillor of The Hague or that the director of the Department for the Preservation of Historic Buildings and Sites is Fons Asselbergs, a former city councillor of Amersfoort. All in all, the government's policies for architecture have created a sound infrastructure designed to help architects on their way. Nearly all the firms in this book have benefited from these institutions.

THE DUTCH IDENTITY
With Dutch architecture of the 1980s marked

by a race to catch up with international trends, it is understandable that at a certain point people began to feel the need for reflection on national traditions and identity and a reassessment of what they might contribute to an international discourse. A crucial moment in this shift of sentiment was the publication of *The Embarrassment of Riches* (1987, appearing in Dutch translation in 1988), a book by the English historian Simon Schama about the culture and mentality of the Dutch sixteenth-century 'Golden Age'.[2]

Schama argued that the foremost social dilemma of the period was how to reconcile wealth with morality, and that this lay at the root of what might be called the national character. He noted that both Calvinism and the humanistic critique of material riches, such as that expressed by Erasmus, had left deep traces in the Dutch mentality, which he argued were still evident in today's society. The Dutch are not normally given to much national introspection, but when an outsider offers an opinion on their collective character they are all the more ready to take him seriously. Schama's book thus attracted wide interest in the Netherlands. The book begins with a motto quoted from John Calvin's *Commentary on Genesis*: 'Let those who have abundance remember that they are surrounded with thorns, and let them take great care not to be pricked by them.' Those living in the Golden Age would have understood this maxim not only as a critique of ostentation and a reminder of its vulnerability to external threats like natural catastrophes or war but as a warning against hubris, which could end in bankruptcy. Indeed, in this sense Calvin's words remain resonant in Dutch culture today. The Netherlands currently enjoys a new period of prosperity, and, as in the Golden Age, it seems that wealth is accompanied by a degree of unease. Now, as then, the discomfort is not just a worry that the prosperous times will fall prey to external hazards but a deeply ingrained Dutch fear, based on historical experience, of overconfidence. The present Social-Democratic premier Wim Kok, a former union leader, is the personification of this concern, and is constantly having to

2. Simon Schama, *The Embarrassment of Riches* (New York, 1987).

defend a strict treasury line and restriction of the national debt, which have consequences for the welfare of the nation in the long run. The collective fear of bankruptcy holds employers and employees in its thrall. Instead of fighting it out over pay rises and working conditions, both sides couch their arguments in terms of the long-term development of the national economy, and they try to achieve a consensus within these parameters. This economic paradigm has become known as the 'polder model'. In some instances the unions have been content to take part in a 'zero round' of their annual pay negotiations in which they do not ask for any pay rise at all.

Calvin's admonition continues to lurk in the background, even in the spheres of architecture, fashion and design. The Dutch spend less on clothing than any other European nation. New buildings are often expected to cost a fraction of what is budgeted in the rest of Europe. The wealthy burghers of the Golden Age built their mansions in the countryside, and when they were in town they played down the size and opulence of their residences. Now, too, the clients for some of the most important country house designs of recent years – OMA's 'Dutch House', for instance, also known as the 'House for Mr. X', or the Möbius House by UN Studio (Ben van Berkel and Caroline Bos) – prefer anonymity.

The echo of Calvin can also be heard when Rem Koolhaas complains that one of the least understood aspects of OMA's work has always been its inexpensiveness. Cheapness has ideological significance for him, partly due to a realization that large parts of the world lack the affluence we take for granted in the West, but partly also due to a concern for the environment. 'It has to do with a sort of minimal use of means. As far as that goes there are indeed two sorts of minimalism: a Calcutta minimalism and a detailed, even fussy minimalism. I feel more affinity with Calcutta…. It absolutely doesn't mean that we only make cheap things, but I think that the research into how you can carry out as many programmes as possible with as little money as possible is incredibly interesting. I think a

building such as Lille Grand Palais that was built with budgets that would also be valid in Calcutta was an interesting project because it proved that you can discard all those fetishes you might use to seduce people and that you can bring about desirable conditions in a specific context purely on the basis of a real commitment. I think that one consequence of the fact that architecture no longer raises the issue of what are great problems of our time means that it is losing credibility. That means that the credibility ends up being displaced onto the object. There is a sort of purely sensual side of architecture that has been almost tragically overestimated as a result.'[3]

Rem Koolhaas is probably most radical in his rejection of an architecture that focuses on aesthetics and the sensuality of detail. But when we compare Dutch architecture, design and fine art of the 1990s with work being done abroad, it is striking that the Dutch output is generally more conceptual, more minimalist, more reduced and more basic; one might say it is *dryer*. Hence the name Droog Design ('Dry Design'), given to a collection of work by mostly young designers selected by the design critic Renny Ramakers and the designer Gijs Bakker, which has been creating a stir in recent years with products that combine standard and semi-finished items in surprising ways and component materials not disguised but made into an explicit feature. The Droog Design collection teeters on the boundary of non-design. Ramakers proposes that the ethos of Droog Design is deeply rooted in the Dutch mentality, and she too refers to the Calvinistic and Erasmian tradition. She observes, however, that Droog Design is paradoxically 'a break with the Dutch design tradition [that] is typically Dutch'.[4] The Droog Design initiative was perhaps originally a product of Dutch culture but it has meanwhile been accorded wider recognition and significance.

A similar process has taken place with respect to Atelier van Lieshout (page 87), whose early work was predominantly a perverse parody of modern Dutch art and design. Gradually, he has constructed a new and autonomous kind of space with conven-

3. Bart Lootsma, *Rem Koolhaas, In search of the new modernity*, Domus 800, January 1998.
4. Renny Ramakers, *Spirit of the Nineties*, in Renny Ramakers, Gijs Bakker (eds), *Droog Design, Spirit of the Nineties* (Rotterdam, 1998).

tions of its own, a realm that he is prepared to defend against the hazards of the outside world, if need be, with armed force. Droog Design and Atelier van Lieshout offer an important key to understanding the enigmatic aesthetics of recent Dutch architecture. Many of the buildings illustrated in this book have been furnished with items from the collection of Droog Design and Atelier van Lieshout. The latter collaborates regularly with OMA.

HOW MODERN IS DUTCH ARCHITECTURE?
The Dutch culture of the 1990s seemed to be very conscious of its own tradition, yet dealt with it in a rather recalcitrant way. It sought the essence of that tradition while reexamining it critically and probing its limits. This was manifest in the symposium that Koolhaas organized under the title 'How Modern is Dutch Architecture?' at the Delft University of Technology in 1990.[5] The participants enthusiastically grappled with the question of how far the Dutch custom of idolizing prewar modernism as a style still bore any relation to the current state of modernity. Apart from the internationally oriented postmodernism that politicians, magazines and such architects as Coenen, Soeters and Uytenhaak embraced in the 1980s, there was a typically Dutch variant, largely sustained by graduates of Delft University of Technology, with representatives including Mecanoo and DKV (Mecanoo refused to participate because they found themselves too good to be criticized by Koolhaas). In the absence of a definable architectural tradition prior to 1990, these firms quoted extensively from the catalogue of modern architecture of the interbellum period and the 1950s, referring symbolically to the social-housing tradition of the 1920s and 1930s. Koolhaas viewed the symposium as a Dutch counterpart to what the communist countries called 'self-criticism', and he did not spare himself. Early work by Koolhaas and OMA, such as the master plan for Amsterdam North (1980–89) and various residential buildings in the Netherlands had drawn extensively on models and examples of Modern architecture. These derivative projects are excluded from Koolhaas's later autobiographical 'novel',

S, M, L, XL.[6] The most devastating appraisal, however, came from the critic Hans van Dijk, who referred to a Dutch 'schoolteachers' modernism', handed down from one generation of lecturers to the next like the priests of a religion with exemplary designs as its icons.[7] 'Schoolteachers' modernism' became a critical cliché in the early 1990s. The Netherlands Architecture Institute picked up the theme and presented it to the outside world as 'Modernism without dogma' and as the official hallmark of Dutch architecture.[8] Official recognition by the Netherlands Architecture Institute sealed the fate of modernism as a faint-hearted option, a superficial style without real substance which many architects were inclined to reject as though it were insipid food or non-alcoholic beer. There were even denigrating remarks about 'yearbook modernism', a reference to the predominating style of work presented in the *Architecture in the Netherlands* yearbook, published by the NAI.[9]

Awakened by Koolhaas, a number of architects steeled themselves to investigate and express a substantive relation to modernism in their work. Shortly before the congress in Delft, Koolhaas himself had set an example in a series of ground-breaking competition entries for the Bibliothèque Nationale de France, the Marine Terminal in Zeebrugge and the Zentrum für Kunst und Medientechnologie in Karlsruhe, Germany. The designs, all dating from 1989, proposed radically new building typologies. In the course of the 1990s Koolhaas elevated radical self-criticism into a method, proceeding step by step in a risk-taking and almost Nietzschean way, systematically bringing all established clichés and accepted certainties into question. Koolhaas became not only the conscience of Dutch architecture but the catalyst of its development.

REM KOOLHAAS
The importance of Rem Koolhaas to the Dutch architecture of the 1990s can scarcely be over-estimated, not least because as long ago as the late 1970s his work had anticipated the crucial changes that were to take place around 1990. His first book, *Delirious New York*

5. Bernard Leupen, Wouter Deen and Christoph Grafe (eds), *Hoe modern is de Nederlandse architectuur?*, 010 Publishers, Rotterdam, 1990.
6. Rem Koolhaas, *S, M, L, XL*, (Rotterdam/New York, 1995).
7. Hans van Dijk, *Het Onderwijzersmodernisme*, in *Hoe*

modern is de Nederlandse architectuur? (Rotterdam, 1990).
8. Hans Ibelings, *Modernisme zonder dogma/Modernism without dogma* (Rotterdam, 1991).
9. *Architecture in the Netherlands* yearbooks: published annually (various eds) (Rotterdam, 1987–).

Droog Design, Tejo Remy
'You can't lay down your memories'
Chest of drawers (1991)

Droog Design, Tejo Remy
Rag Chair (1991)

Droog Design, Dick van Hoff
'Stop' tap (1991)

Droog Design, Rody Graumans
85 Lamps (1993)

Droog Design, Marcel Wanders
Knotted Chair (1996)

(1970), depicted a society marked by radical congestion and hedonistic individualism in a metropolis that was then already part of an international capitalist network.[10] His 1971 study on the Berlin Wall and his *Exodus* project of 1972 had envisaged the fall of the Berlin Wall which took place in 1989, inaugurating the almost total global ascendancy of capitalism.[11] In other words, from an early stage in his career, Koolhaas was on the scent of a new brand of modernity, the first signs of which were only just becoming detectable. This pioneering aspect of OMA's work was perhaps obscured during the 1980s by the more traditionally modernist look of most of the firm's designs, but when we study the plans' organizations, the innovations are clear, particularly those of the unrealized projects.

But a new modernity must in its early years necessarily ensconce itself in the shell of its predecessor, much as a city dweller might look for an old country farmhouse to convert into a weekend home. The relationship between tradition and innovation is well illustrated by Koolhaas's design for renovation of the nineteenth-century panopticon prison building in Arnhem (1979–81). Although the design was not executed, other Dutch panopticon prisons were subsequently renovated according to the principles that OMA proposed. Moreover, Koolhaas's analysis of the Arnhem building prompted a complete reversal of thinking about the construction of new prisons in the Netherlands.[12] Another example is the urban design for the IJ-Plein district in Amsterdam-Noord, built between 1980 and 1989. Just after the democratization vogue of the 1970s, OMA faced a situation in which they had to deal not only with the client and the city but with the inhabitants of adjoining districts and future residents. Many urban development schemes foundered at this time because of such constraints. What tended to happen was that the designer presented his plan and the residents criticized it so harshly that he had to start all over again, a process that was capable of endless repetition. To circumvent this problem, instead of submitting a finished design, OMA took to turning up with a briefcase full of urban

designs, which they introduced in a standardized format. If the residents had specific wishes for the new housing scheme, the architects could immediately inform them of the consequences for its feasibility without first having to prepare yet another design. The eventual design was thus the outcome of a process of negotiation that proceeded with surprising smoothness.

Many of OMA's plans aimed at achieving greater living density produce a melting pot of different programmes and lifestyles that allows or even compels people to construct their own identity instead of taking it as something predetermined. The designs are social condensers, but unlike the schemes of Soviet Russia in the 1920s, they are not meant to generate a uniform society – just the opposite. The density and melting pot OMA envisioned are now a reality: the majority of the world's population lives in cities and free-market capitalism has become a global condition – above all in the Netherlands.

The old building typologies were poorly adapted to this new condition, and OMA's greatest achievement has been to develop a whole range of new ones. In particular, the continuous folded floor as a seamless continuation of the earth's surface, an idea that OMA launched in their competition design of the public library of Jussieu in Paris, has been adopted in variant form by numerous architectural practices. A multitude of former OMA employees, including Kees Christiaanse, Dobbelaar, De Kovel/De Vroom (DKV), Willem Jan Neutelings, and Winy Maas and Jacob van Rijs of MVRDV, now have successful practices of their own in which they continue to develop the ideas of OMA. But Koolhaas is also a role model for countless other Dutch architects who realize the importance in a rapidly changing society of undertaking their own research and theoretical work. Many of them also recognize that it is possible to make a feature of these activities, to raise the the profile of their practices or even engage in 'branding' their work. Exemplary figures include Wiel Arets, UN Studio, Erick van Egeraat, West 8 (Adriaan Geuze) and NOX (Lars Spuybroek).

10. Rem Koolhaas, *Delirious New York* (New York/London,1978).
11. Rem Koolhaas, 'Exodus, The Berlin Wall, Field Trip', in *S, M, L, XL* (Rotterdam/New York, 1995).

12. Ibid., in 'Revision'.

Adriaan Geuze/West 8
Development of the Randstad
Land reclamation, 13th-15th centuries   17th-18th centuries

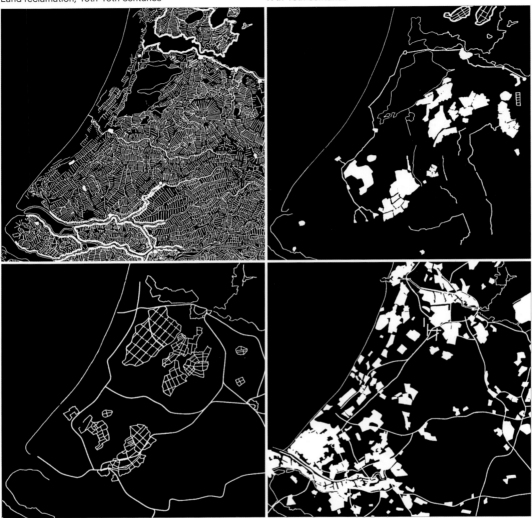

19th century   20th century

THE 'SECOND MODERNITY'

It has become increasingly clear that the foundations for a second phase of modernity that would largely dictate the course of architecture in the 1990s were laid in the 1970s and 1980s. This second modernity is, according to sociologists Ulrich Beck and Anthony Giddens, a product of global economic and political developments, of the rise of international media networks, of new forms of democracy based on systems of expertise and the political involvement of individual citizens and, not least, of congestion.[13] While the first phase of modernity was largely shaped by the industrial revolution and its consequences, the second phase is an outcome of the rise of electronics and communications technology. As a small trading nation and prosperous welfare state, the Netherlands is perhaps more susceptible to these developments than other countries and therefore forced to anticipate the developing situation, among other things at a political level. The unification of Europe has played an important part in this because of policies committed to developing open markets. The required process of deregulation has obliged the Dutch government to abolish, privatize or otherwise change countless public and semi-public agencies, subsidies and laws.

An important byproduct of this process that has significantly affected architecture occurred when the official subsidies for social housing construction were terminated in 1994. The housing corporations that formerly commissioned projects on a non-profit basis all had their debts annulled, and have had to operate as independent property developers on the free market without government support ever since. This took an important instrument for planning out of government hands. In the same period, however, the central government calculated that between 800,000 and 1,000,000 new homes would be needed by 2005. This is a huge number in its own right, but as the market demand is principally for single-family houses with gardens, new developments will devour a much larger area of land than they would have done under the old system, which virtually allowed the government to decree high-rise

construction. The price of land and the expense of preparing it for building are rising steeply, but at the same time the Dutch are suddenly revealing a collective wish to keep their views of the landscape open and unobstructed. The upshot is that the new housing estates will have unprecedented compactness and density and include a reduced, if not minimal, amount of public space.

These schemes will change the face of the Netherlands, despite the grand but old-fashioned plans to build a new town of 50,000 to 100,000 homes on land reclaimed from the sea just off the shore of The Hague and Rotterdam (known as the Waterman Plan), and to create a new suburban island called IJburg in the IJsselmeer lake near Amsterdam. It is the 'green heart', a largely agricultural area in the middle of the ring formed by the Randstad towns of Amsterdam, Utrecht, Gouda, Rotterdam, The Hague and Haarlem, that will bear the brunt of the new development. Every government paper expresses a desire to preserve this rural zone, but changing conditions are making agriculture unprofitable. The green area is under threat not only from the major expansion schemes of the surrounding towns, notably Utrecht, but also from the countless individual houses being built in odd spots everywhere.

Since the 1990s, it has no longer been the government that takes the lead in the debate surrounding these issues but the architects and town planners themselves. In 1995, Adriaan Geuze and West 8 erected a gigantic model consisting of 800,000 tiny wooden houses in the arcade of the Netherlands Architecture Institute. The effect was shocking because the implications the new housing boom could have for town and country suddenly became clear: a landscape with an endless sea of houses, recalling certain megacities in North and South America. From an urban planning viewpoint, the model made it manifest that organization of the homes into separate neighbourhoods was irrelevant; it would remain an enormous, undifferentiated sea of houses. The latter effect was further underlined in a small book, *In Holland staat een huis*, written by West 8, which showed

13. Ulrich Beck, Anthony Giddens, Scott Lash *et al.*
Reflexive Modernization, Politics, Tradition and Aesthetics in the Modern Social Order
(Cambridge/Oxford, 1994/1995).

Adriaan Geuze/West 8
Model of '800,000 Houses'
Netherlands Architecture Institute, Rotterdam (1995)

dozens of tactically photographed housing developments from the 1970s and 1980s.[14] Although the planners and architects had invariably done their best to give each neighbourhood a unique identity, it was that very attempt that had resulted in an overwhelming sense of uniformity. The Federation of Dutch Town Planners subsequently issued a large map, 'De Nieuwe Kaart van Nederland', marked with all the building plans throughout the Netherlands. It demonstrated how important it was going to be to coordinate the developments at a higher level. So far, not much has happened in this respect.

MAPPING THE FORCE FIELDS
Paradoxically, it is these difficult circumstances that have challenged architects to create provocative and radical new plans. Predictably it has often been relatively young architects who have produced designs of this kind, for they were able to start with a clean slate when the architectural climate changed so rapidly in the first half of the 1990s. The current widespread interest in the work of these young architects is not unconnected with the fact that the generation that rebelled in the 1960s and 1970s now occupies key positions in the architectural profession and in politics. The audacity of the young architects appeals to them and in many cases the older generation themselves are prepared to take risks and participate in experiments. Those architects – often only a little older – who were prominent in the 1980s were much more inclined to stress the problems and dangers of a new situation and to put up a resistance by clinging on to their own innovations. After all, their work was a reaction to the technocratic approach of the 1960s and the socio-political philosophy of the 1970s, in which the creativity of the individual citizen was taken seriously. For these architects, there was a strong belief in architecture's autonomous tradition as a bulwark of high culture. This is problematic, however, in the present situation, in which the architect can no longer rely on that autonomous history because the authority and power which the traditional architect of cathedrals and palaces had to implement his ideas no longer exists.

The architect must now justify himself to many different parties, the client, building contractors and engineers, future residents and users, residents of neighbouring areas who insist on consultation and the municipality. The architect must comply with countless laws and ordinances that are often contradictory. They must continually devise new strategies to continue playing a significant part in this situation and are forever entering into new alliances with the various parties involved in the plans rendering the process long and slow. For every project the architect must study the power relationships within which it exists and create ways of manipulating them. There is no longer any question of architectural autonomy.
In the second modernity, the Dutch tradition of consultation has become wholly institutionalized. It could be regarded as teamwork – it is not the chairperson's place to force through a personal opinion. If even one of the interested parties withholds consent, the whole process could be delayed even further by the legal or political actions which are available to the other parties. Once a consensus has been achieved, however, the way is open to rapid and decisive action. But concessions have had to be made, and although the results may be strikingly good, more often they are equivocal. The crucial factor is the quality and credibility of the arguments deployed and the way the architect has integrated these into the scheme.
Firms like OMA, West 8, MVRDV, Neutelings Riedijk and UN Studio try to deal with the new situation by plunging into it with almost masochistic gusto. They analyze the context of each project afresh, without entertaining prior assumptions, and try to bring its inherent potential to light. Very often, the process starts with an effort to map all possible internal and external forces that could play some significant part in the project's execution. This practice also influences theoretical development more strongly than in other countries, where the formation of theory is chiefly an academic affair. Willem Jan Neutelings has provocatively described this as 'laziness', since he argues that ideally the design should arise almost of its own accord from the boundary conditions.[15] The truth is,

14. Adriaan Geuze and West 8, *In Holland staat een huis* (Rotterdam, 1995).

15. Willem Jan Neutelings, 'Over de luiheid, recyclage, sculpturale wiskunde envernuftigheid', in Bernard Colenbrander (ed.), *Mutaties* (Rotterdam, 1996).

of course, more complicated than that – there was perhaps a tongue-in-cheek element to Neutelings's pronouncement – however, a certain common signature can be detected among all the architects concerned. Van Berkel and Bos speak of 'mobile forces', and MVRDV coined the term 'datascapes'.[16] Although the work produced by these firms differs widely, these labels aptly characterize the new situation. Van Berkel and Bos try to collect all possible information relating to a project, and then use the computer's power to synthesize it to create a 'diagram' that then forms the basis of the design. The datascapes of MVRDV, on the other hand, are rather like elaborated versions of what used to be called the 'situation' of the design. The situation was understood to mean the physical place where the design was to be embedded into the existing morphology. Nowadays, however, many more intangible factors have a bearing on the architectural situation, including the planning envelope, laws and regulations on the allowance of natural light and potential noise nuisance, constructional requirements and the needs and wishes of users and neighbouring residents. MVRDV visualizes the outcome of these factors in standardized diagrams or datascapes. Again using computers datascapes are then superimposed on one another – mapped – to reveal the project's constraints before the negotiation process is started up with those involved. This approach ultimately leads to a design in which different layers and fractures within the process remain visible. Datascapes can be extrapolated to a larger scale, to theoretical exercises about the growth of cities, in which the consequences of future scenarios can be visually investigated.[17]

Whatever the merits of such strategies, by developing them the architect succeeds in preserving a certain measure of control over the project, not in a visionary or authoritarian manner, but as a manager who keeps the process on track – although often not without a personal agenda. The most important quest at present is undoubtedly the maximum differentiation of typologies, with the aim of responding to the problems posed by an ever more differentiated society, a theme that clearly plays an important part in town planning, in housing construction, public buildings and offices in many ways. This search is paralleled by research into new forms of organization, in which transparency and connectivity battle for priority.

At a more abstract level, the personal agenda is not infrequently also influenced by philosophers – Foucault, Derrida, Lyotard, Deleuze, to name a few – although never as emphatically as in the Anglo-Saxon architectural discourse. Ben van Berkel and Caroline Bos, and Lars Spuybroek come closest to the latter and participate explicitly in that discourse. The main difference between these and other Dutch architectural practices is that they seem to be far more interested in the internal coherence of their designs. Their work nonetheless shows serious attention to the need for finding practical solutions to the complex problems of contemporary society. A typical instance of this is the special issue of the New York publication *Any* magazine, entitled 'Diagram Work', for which van Berkel and Bos acted as guest editors. In their introduction they write that the point of departure for their research into the diagram was the observation that 'the repetitive process of the verifying of knowledge deeply inhibits the practice of architecture' and is thereby a threat to architecture's future. 'In order to avoid total disillusionment and exhaustion, architecture must continue to evolve its internal discourse, to adapt in specific ways to new materials and technological innovations, and to engage in constant self-analysis…. The end of the grand narrative does not mean that architects no longer dream their own dreams, different from anyone else's.'[18]

It is thus clear that despite all the potential problems facing Dutch architecture, it enjoys a lively discourse in which practical, political and aesthetic arguments go hand in hand with national traditions and international references. The most important result so far is that a series of interesting and innovative buildings and projects have been built.

16. Ben van Berkel, *Mobile Forces* (Berlin, 1994); Winy Maas, *Datascape: The Final Extravaganza,* in *Daidalos* 69/70, Dec 1998/Jan 1999.
17. MVRDV, *Metacity/Datatown* (Rotterdam, 1999).

18. Ben van Berkel and Caroline Bos, preface to '*Diagram Work*', *Any* magazine, no. 23 (New York, 1998).

Academy of Arts and Architecture, Maastricht
Studio building by night

WIEL ARETS

Academy of Arts and Architecture, Maastricht
Site plan

The architecture of Wiel Arets is riddled with paradoxes. It presents a hard, remorseless appearance within the urban context, yet does its best to be invisible. Interior spaces are compellingly stage-managed but actually aim to create sanctuaries for self-regulating populations. Photogenic though it may be, it is really an 'architecture without qualities', rather like M. Teste, the only fictional character ever created by Arets's favourite author, Paul Valéry. As such his designs are the expression of a longing for invisibility.

Arets belongs to a generation of architects who were trained in the late 1970s and early 1980s, when postmodernism was enjoying its showy heyday. Shrugging off postmodernism from the outset, he has been more interested in philosophical aspects, in an architecture based on what can perhaps be best described as *a presence of mind* – a lucidity that knows no certainties, alert, mobile and sharply self-aware. Arets comes from a background in which architecture is unequivocally an autonomous discipline, and his work has developed steadily in the direction of a practice in which non-architectural, 'softer' and less tangible aspects play an important part. It is an architecture which at first seems simple but on second glance discloses richness and poetry, and thus aims in the long run to instigate processes of transformation. It is an architecture whose fragmentary but simultaneously essayistic character is precise and to the point, yet it still leaves room for individual interpretation and imagination.

Arets's designs invariably take the form of strongly reduced geometric bodies embedded into an urban context. As compositions of blocks and bars, they are inserted into aerial photographs or scale models, which themselves show a fascinating morphological complexity. In this respect they bear a resemblance to the designs of Giorgio Grassi, which appear as simple blocks in topographical maps, and to those of Tadao Ando. Unlike Grassi, Arets does not try from the outset to reconcile the hardness of his designs with history: the reconciliation will inevitably come later, through the action of time. Time will age the materials, which Arets prefers to leave untreated, making his buildings look less aggressive and blending them into their contexts. But time will also allow for shifts inside the buildings as they are gradually appropriated by their users. Arets is conscious too that changes will take place in the surroundings of his buildings over time. He stresses the importance of these processes in his prolific writing, in which he frequently uses metaphors of the body. He refers, for example, to his buildings as prostheses that replace obsolete parts of the city; he writes of cuts in the skin of the earth that leave scars; and he mentions viral processes that are set in motion by his architecture. In his essay 'An Alabaster Skin', Arets writes that architecture is violent because it refuses to be a victim of its surroundings, but at the same time can bend the context to its will precisely because it is its victim: '[Architecture] can only become part of the world by entering into marriage with its surroundings. . . . Marriage has lent it cunning.'

The skins of Arets's buildings are simultaneously part of the skin of the city and the skin of whatever takes place inside the building, a membrane through which Arets continually plays with different grades of transparency to make the tension between inside and outside, between private and public, productive. His interiors are usually characterized by generously open ground plans, within which heterotopias can develop. The internal structure also features coercive circulation routes, which conduct the pedestrian past a series of significant spaces and vistas, offering them a cinematic experience.

The most radical example of Wiel Arets's approach to architecture must inevitably be his Academy of Art and Architecture (1989–93) in Maastricht. It comprises two sections joined by a raised footbridge that passes between the tops of several oak trees. The bridge forms a gateway to a former city-centre industrial site that has been transformed into a residential urban square. One section of the building, which is partly submerged below ground, contains public spaces, such as an auditorium, library and canteen. One circulation route leads to the roof and over the footbridge to the second section of the building, which is also partly beneath ground level. Here, large, loft-like spaces house the studios in which future artists can mark out their own territories. The façades of both sections are clad in glass bricks creating narrow windows that offer the users inside an outdoor view but do not let outsiders peer in. The passer-by has no hint of the activities taking place inside until night falls and the building's interior is illuminated and transformed into a giant lantern wedged into the fabric of the city.

The offices for the insurance company AZL (1990–95) in Heerlen, are implanted into an existing block like an appendage, with large parts of the original structure being retained. The building forms a new liaison between two streets and keeps the structure of the historic courtyard gardens of the city intact. Arets developed a new office furniture system for the large, open-plan office interiors, and a system that offers the users privacy but does not impose fixed work locations. On arriving in the office, employees simply plug their laptops and telephones into an available socket.

Arets's most elaborate game of hide-and-seek is played in the design of the police station in Vaals, where the three volumes that make up the building correspond to different levels of contact between the police staff and members of the public. The volume adjoining the pedestrian route that passes the building contains the areas in which contact between the police and the public is at a maximum: a duty desk, a glass cabinet displaying a collection of police headgear from various countries, and interview and interrogation rooms, as well as the cell block and the kennels (from where the police dogs can bark at approaching visitors). The middle volume houses a central control room and changing rooms for uniformed officers going on duty. From here, they can enter the most protected part of the building: the offices, crisis room and canteen, which features a transparent wall through which the

Academy of Arts and Architecture, Maastricht
Interior of footbridge

Academy of Arts and Architecture, Maastricht
Basement of studio block

contents of the changing room's lockers are visible. The entire building, poised to look vigilantly out over the surrounding South-Limburg countryside, is draped in a skin of frosted glass through which the window openings of the inner wall can be glimpsed: behind this layer, some of the interior glimmers through, particularly when the inside is lit at night. The building's simple, stern concept gives it at first sight the appearance of an ordinary office building, but the perturbing equivocation of the façade and the veiled gleam of the insulating material behind it make it convincing. In the multilayered transparency of its walls, the police station faithfully reflects the ambivalent character of a police force – on the one hand open and people-friendly but on the other committed to supervision and enforcement.

AZL Pensionfund Building, Heerlen
Main entrance

AZL Pensionfund Building, Heerlen
Restaurant

AZL Pensionfund Building, Heerlen
Elevation at entrance zone

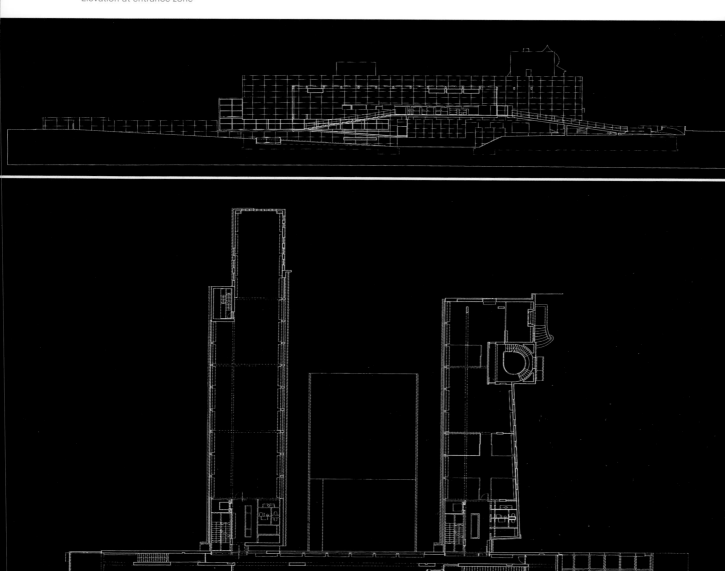

AZL Pensionfund Building, Heerlen
Ground plan, entrance level

AZL Pensionfund Building, Heerlen
Entrance with sunken car park

AZL Pensionfund Building, Heerlen
View from conference room of environmental façade

AZL Pensionfund Building, Heerlen
Patio of directors' room

Police Station, Vaals
Site and ground-floor plans

Police Station, Vaals
Rear elevation

Police Station, Vaals
Waiting area for interview rooms

Police Station, Cuijck
Ground-floor plan

Third-floor plan

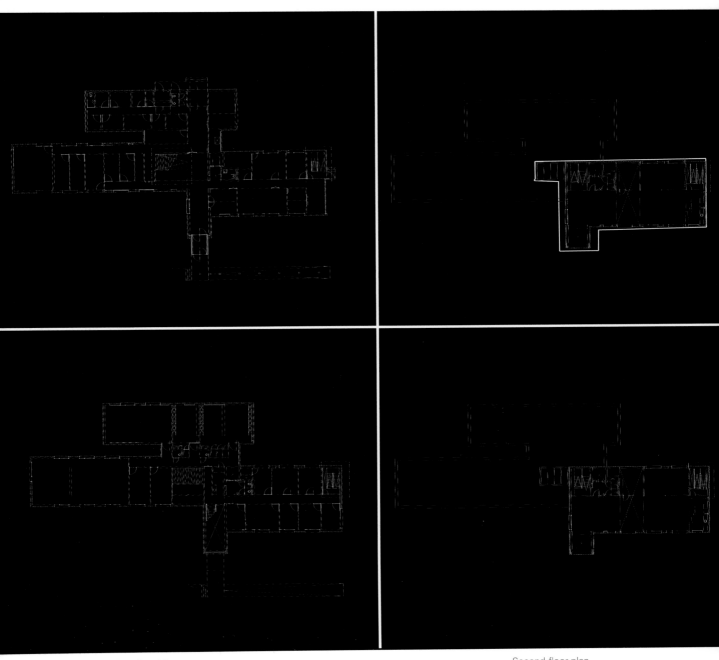

First-floor plan

Second-floor plan

Police Station, Cuijck
Front façade

Police Station, Cuijck
Glass wall detail

Police Station, Cuijck
Interior corridor

Karbouw Building, Amersfoort
Side elevation

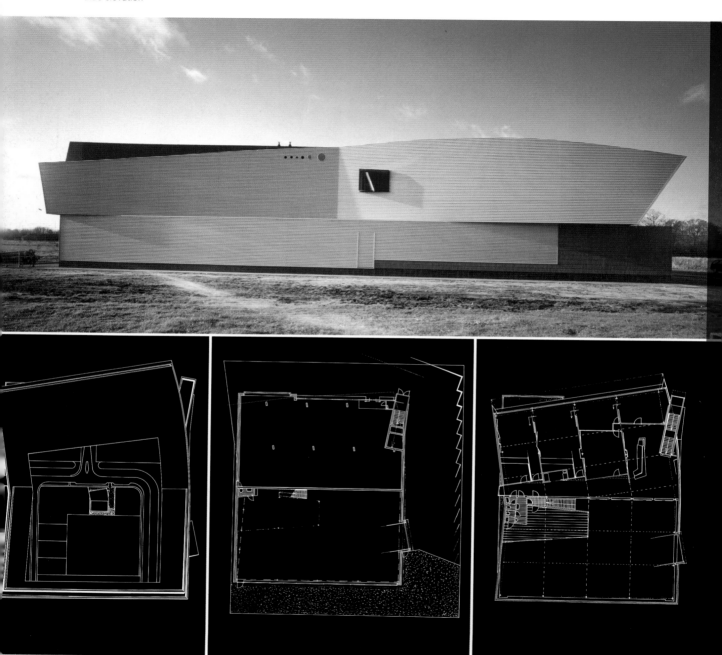

Karbouw Building, Amersfoort
Plans

River Waal and the surrounding polders, it is a location rich in Roman and medieval remains, including remnants of a city wall and a twelfth-century fort. The museum borders one side of a large public square beneath which there is an underground car park. In its glazed façade the building is not really a visual boundary so much as a mirage reflecting the ever-changing sky and the trees. The public space continues into the building, where an immensely broad and lazy staircase proceeds through a wide gallery, with views of the medieval city wall, up to the museum rooms on the upper floor. The spectacular staircase is the central structuring element of the museum interior and gives access to the library, cafeteria, auditorium and educational section on the ground floor, and to the cloakroom, an archaeological installation and exhibition rooms in the basement. The upper floor rooms have a neutral atmosphere and contain an arrangement of partitions that allow the visitor to take different routes through changing displays of the collections. The rooms are topped by an undulating ceiling of aluminium slats, recalling designs by Alvar Aalto.

Van Berkel's most recent projects feature the use of computers in the design process at an earlier stage. In an urban planning scheme for the area around the main railway station of Arnhem, currently in development, a computer model was used at the initial design stage to quantify traffic flows, which were represented as tubes of varying width and connectivity. The wishes of a wide array of involved parties were then modelled as force-fields acting on and deforming these tubes. The resulting form is not something that has sprung in its entirety from the architect's brain, but indeed incorporates all the 'mobile forces' that society exerts in an inclusive, dynamic diagram.

Möbius House
Perspective in wooded setting

Möbius House
Living room detail

Möbius House
Ground-level plan

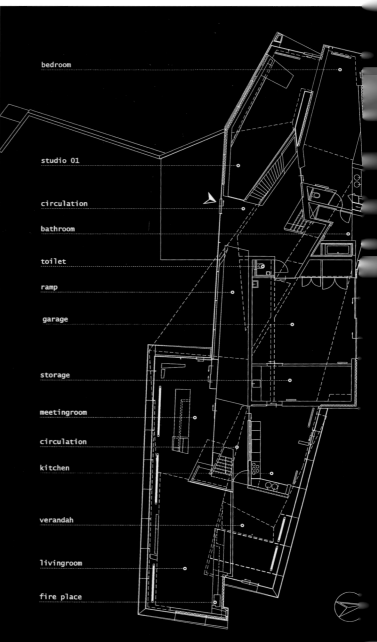

bedroom

studio 01

circulation

bathroom

toilet

ramp

garage

storage

meetingroom

circulation

kitchen

verandah

livingroom

fire place

Möbius House
Living room view

STUDIO

Möbius House
Lower-level plan

Möbius House
Roof plan

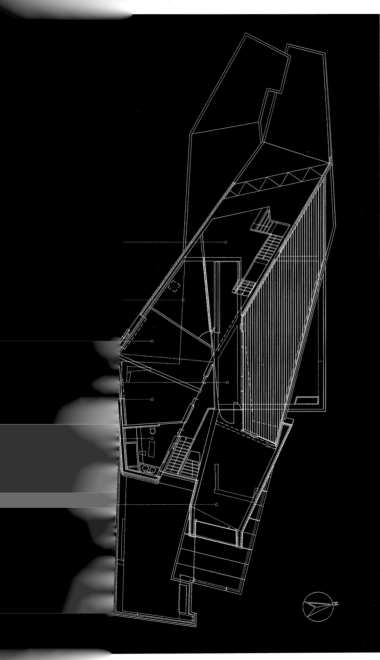

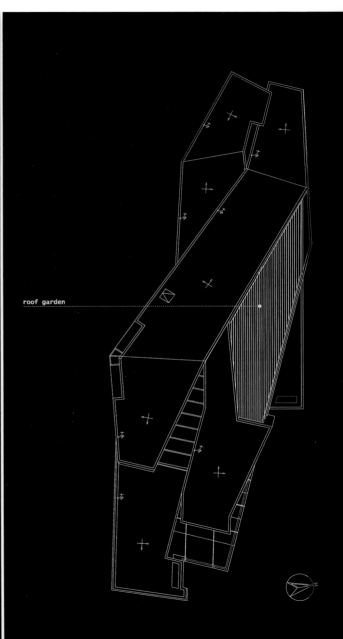

roof garden

Museum Het Valkhof, Nijmegen

Cross section at entrance
zone

First floor

Ground floor

Basement

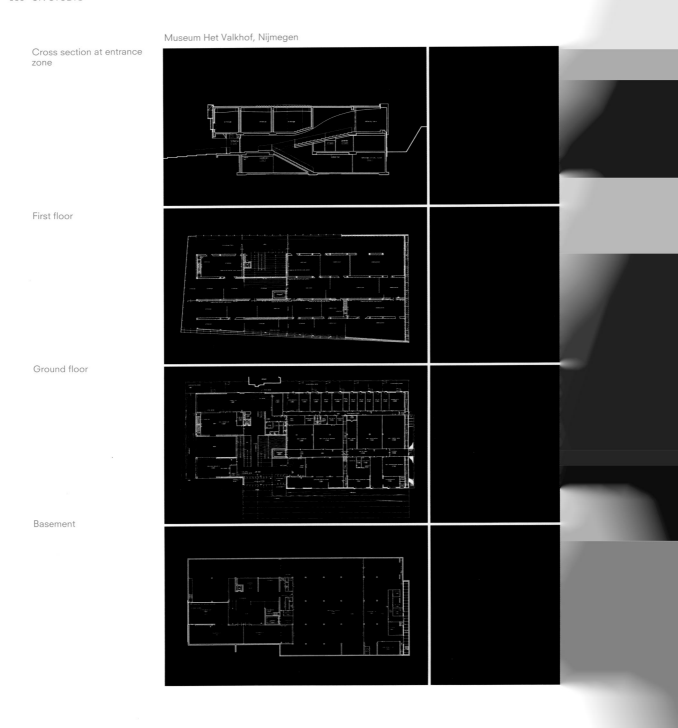

Museum Het Valkhof, Nijmegen
View from public plaza

Museum Het Valkhof, Nijmegen
Entrance stairwell

Museum Het Valkhof, Nijmegen
Gallery

ING/Nationale Nederlanden Building, Budapest
Roofscape view

071
ERICK VAN EGERAAT

ING/Nationale Nederlanden Building, Budapest
Interior of 'spaceship' boardroom

ING/Nationale Nederlanden Building, Budapest
Exterior view of 'spaceship' boardroom

ING/Nationale Nederlanden Building, Budapest
Meeting area in 'spaceship'

Erick van Egeraat began his career working for Mecanoo (page 103), where he was a founder member and one of its main designers, before starting his own firm in 1995. A few of the projects shown here were partly designed during the transitional period between the two firms. Although unsurprisingly there are similarities between the work of Mecanoo and that of van Egeraat's independent studio, there are also distinct differences. While van Egeraat embraces modernism and thinks strongly in terms of atmospheres, he is much more pronounced and unconventional in this respect than his previous firm. He does not shrink from vehemence. His work can be immensely quiet, as in his Nature Museum in Rotterdam, or extremely inexpensive, as in his Technical High School in Utrecht; qualities that are explicit in the designs. Paradoxically, the explicit cheapness of the school results in a sense of quality similar to the extravagant baroque of his design for the ING Bank in Budapest. Baroque – sumptuous and voluptuous – is closest to van Egeraat's heart, but it does not exclude alternative approaches.

This attitude is apparent from the book he has produced about his work, *Six Ideas About Architecture* (1997), an exuberant publication with different typefaces and colours that mix and overlap. Van Egeraat reveals that he is sceptical about theorization because it can lead to a debate with mutually exclusive standpoints. 'I don't understand the thinking. Concentrating on the opposite ends of the spectrum doesn't solve anything …. Architecture is more than a matter of absolutes, more than a case of being one thing rather than another. Architecture is both/and, not either/or. It is inclusive, not exclusive. It is about a range of possibilities rather than simple-minded certainties.' But for some, the strategy, tone or atmosphere to be adopted for a project depends on the context, for van Egeraat it is an intuitive choice: 'I want architecture to be fashionable. Architecture is really only about taste.'

The building with which van Egeraat launched his career as an independent architect was the ING Bank and Nationale Nederlanden Insurance building in Budapest (1992–1997). The essence of this project was a reconciliation of opposites, it was perhaps the ideal commission for van Egeraat – the offices of a modern banking and insurance company from the Netherlands, pioneering the growth of capitalism in a former communist country – a very different proposition from erecting a building in a country where practically everything is already established and where only marginal improvements can be made. It was moreover the first time that the insurers and the bankers, who have quite different priorities, would be sharing an office following the merger of the two companies. Insurers are salespeople at heart, but bankers seek to convey reliability, solidity and tradition. These oppositions are expressed in the design, which involved the conversion of a monumental historic building from the period of the Danube Monarchy. The original building was in part meticulously restored, in part radically added to. The bank section was allotted a

ING/Nationale Nederlanden Building, Budapest
Top floor with restaurant and underside of 'spaceship'

boardroom in the former salon, a space with a splendid *Jugendstil* ceiling whose decoration continues over the walls. Van Egeraat designed furniture and new wainscoting specially for this room. The insurers, on the other hand, were given a modern boardroom in a remarkable organic form, reminiscent of Lebbeus Woods, that seems to float above the staircase and rest atop the roof. The contrasts in atmosphere between old and new, between the bank and the insurance company, between the subterranean basement and the airy glass roof that turns the former courtyard into an atrium, were harmonized by a consistent pursuit of refined detailing in all parts; the soft and hard furnishings are also van Egeraat's choice. The result is a spectacular, radiant design that can be seen as a background in several advertising clips. At the rear of the remodelled building an extention was added later, which has a subtly reflective skin, part of which is executed with differing panes of special glass. The resulting façade mirrors the surrounding historic buildings and diminishes the impairment to the existing building.

The Nature Museum in Rotterdam is of an entirely different order. It also involved the remodelling and extension of a historic building, a villa dating from 1851. To avoid competing for attention with the museum's exhibits, the detailed design has a radical minimalism. A glass hall facing the neighbouring KunstHAL (designed by OMA), gives an outside glimpse of the museum's contents. On the upper floor, a horizontally elongated window admits light from above. A similar window set low in the wall downstairs opens up the vista of the Museumpark.

The Technical High School in Utrecht is yet again different in character. There was already an existing design when the city invited van Egeraat to become involved in the project, and he made use of it to a large extent. This was applicable to the remarkably pragmatic fenestration of the façades. Van Egeraat elevated the chief problem affecting the project – an insufficient budget – to a positive design aesthetic. The building's interior has an extremely austere finish in exposed concrete. The exterior made use of a very low-priced multilayered façade through which the mineral fibre insulation remains visible. At one corner of the building is the entrance lobby, a simple glass box with an airy environment that is half-way between an exterior and interior condition. Inside this large volume, the auditorium is raised on stilts, with a simple wooden reception kiosk alongside it. The result is an interesting but ostensibly casual composition of volumes and open spaces. The mounting of fluorescent lighting tubes behind the translucent corrugated cladding of the auditorium marks the school's entrance area with an intriguing beacon that can be seen from afar.

ING/Nationale Nederlanden Building, Budapest
Atrium

ING/Nationale Nederlanden Building, Budapest
Section

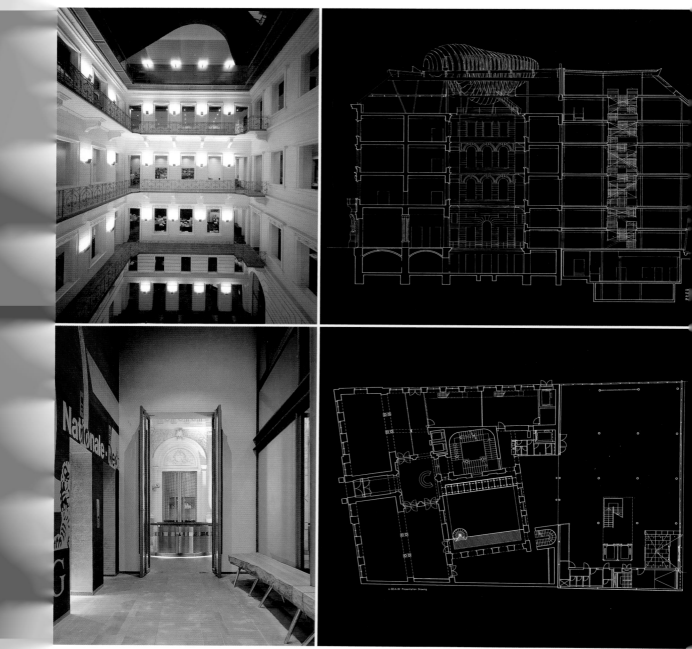

ING/Nationale Nederlanden Building, Budapest
Entrance to insurance company office with waiting room

ING/Nationale Nederlanden Building, Budapest
Ground floor

Nature Museum, Rotterdam
Elevation on park side

Nature Museum, Rotterdam
Front elevation of new building

Nature Museum, Rotterdam
Site plan showing relationship to KunstHAL by OMA (below)

Nature Museum, Rotterdam
Plans

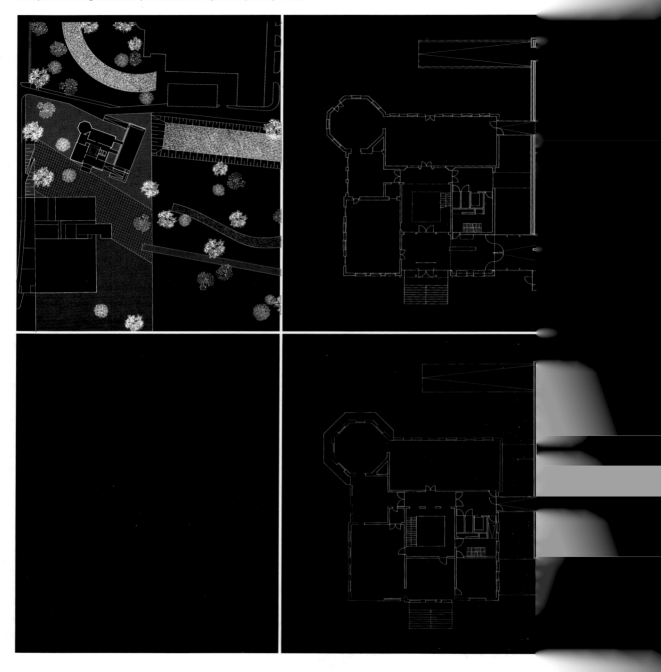

Nature Museum, Rotterdam
Interior

Nature Museum, Rotterdam
Interior detail

Technical High School, Utrecht
Exterior view

Technical High School, Utrecht
Site and floor plans

Modular Mobile Home, Skull Room, Information Stand
Installation view, Galerie Fons Welters, Amsterdam (1996)

ATELIER VAN LIESHOUT

Much of what artist Joep van Lieshout has produced (in a relatively short time) does not consist of art in the strictest sense, but of utensils, items of furniture, architecture and articles of food and drink – 'practical solutions for everyday problems', as he puts it, with a heavy dose of irony. The irony is appropriate because Atelier van Lieshout has a sharp eye for the underside of modernity. For a long time the project of modernity was viewed as a civilizing process, but increasingly this has proved an illusion. In his view, the violence that was once an everyday part of human existence is concealed in modern society. It used to be that a pig might be slaughtered in a village and afterwards there would be a feast, but today the killing is banished to hermetically sealed slaughterhouses on the edge of the city. Once people used to die at home and were laid out there. Now death takes place in the sterile, anonymous surroundings of a hospital on the city outskirts. Such areas have also become the site for cemeteries (for people and cars), allotments and trailer parks.

Atelier van Lieshout is situated in just such a spot in the Rotterdam docks, a place where everything that the city cannot stomach is dumped: grimy little businesses with premises in gasometers or dilapidated sheds, piles of stinking hides on the street waiting to be tanned, second-hand car lots, do-it-yourself emporiums and cheap studio space for artists. The studio's office overlooks site set up by the municipality for streetwalkers, a kind of parking area where women or transsexuals are picked up by men in cars; wooden partitions are provided so that they can have sex. The area was established to lure the sex trade away from the city centre, which the council recognised as being too confrontational and too much of a nuisance for residents.

Recently Atelier van Lieshout itself has started slaughtering animals. The meat is preserved in the traditional professional manner and the studio has installed tables, troughs and ovens. The studio also distills its own alcohol. The products are consumed by the members of the studio, and also exhibited and sold. The main feature of most of Atelier van Lieshout's work is that it can be used. The studio produces furniture, toilet fittings, trailers, bathrooms, kitchens, building extensions and complete interiors, as well as contributing to projects by OMA, such as the lamps of the Educatorium in Utrecht (page 182) and the bars and toilets in the Congrexpo in Lille (page 191).

Atelier van Lieshout's activities aim to cast doubt on a number of conventions in the arts; but they are also a challenge to architects and designers. Van Lieshout's furniture looks distinctly like the cheap modern items one can buy in large furniture outlets, yet there is a significant difference. While mass-market items of furniture are made of plasticized chipboard that is often disguised to resemble another material – an expensive wood, for instance – the crude fibreglass texture of van Lieshout's furniture does not pretend to be anything other than plastic. This honesty, this lack of shame, is the aesthetic statement Atelier van Lieshout makes, and a number of provocative questions are raised. What, after all,

Toilets, baths, washbasins, polyester
Exhibition Ateliers '63, Palais des Beaux Arts, Brussels (1998)

could be better than cheap furniture that is even washable? What are we supposed to do with all those meaningless *objets d'art* that are ornamental rather than functional? What's wrong with producing designs in an unlimited series? In a society dominated by mass production, can the value of an art work still be defined by its uniqueness? And does that art work have to be made by the artist alone? Could it not also be produced by a company such as Atelier van Lieshout? Is it not all to the common good if clever do-it-yourself enthusiasts can copy the work at home with the aid of the manuals provided by the artist? Paradoxically, it is questions like these in the context of cultural discourse that elevate van Lieshout's work to the status of art.

The crudity of van Lieshout's art works is a calculated insult to architects and artists, who try to produce objects that are as refined as possible. This is because van Lieshout's work is shown primarily in museums and galleries and thus, as Marcel Duchamp proved, the object has a cultural value by contextual definition. Van Lieshout's work is also cheaper than the work of most architects and artists. And precisely because it is art, it does not need to conform to conventional requirements. The boundaries have become blurred, so that it can be difficult to decide whether van Lieshout's work is art or just a collection of useful objects. For example, some of the items of jewelry van Lieshout makes are in the form of weapons – among them a hybrid object somewhere between a pistol and a knuckle-duster and a Rambo knife – and have more than once been confiscated by the authorities; lawsuits are still pending in Holland and America. But this has not prevented van Lieshout from developing a cannon that can be mounted on a pickup truck.

More important than the fact that Atelier van Lieshout is stretching and subverting the limits of what is called art is the fact that the work constantly harries modernism and in doing so exposes its darker aspects. Van Lieshout's indifference to the aesthetic and moral sides of his work is not unqualified, because it is specifically this indifferent quality that gives his images and his artistry such an impudent power. It is an *active* indifference, such as Georges Bataille saw in the work of Eduard Manet. Bataille believed that Manet's painting rejected every expression of higher awareness or deeper meaning. This is not to say that Manet's paintings are meaningless, but that he painted an absence of meaning that was characteristic of his time. By stripping that characteristic bare, according to Bataille, Manet achieved a radical liberation: the same is true of van Lieshout.

It is a simplistic argument to suggest that van Lieshout's work is an extension of the radical architecture of the 1970s, which celebrated do-it-yourself building and the desire for independence and self-determination. While van Lieshout is particularly interested in the hippies who build energy-saving homes from waste products of the consumer society, and he is fascinated by the simplicity, purity and autonomy of groups like the Amish and the Shakers of America, he is also aware that people are driven by noble

intentions, but also by their passions. This can be seen in the blatant sexuality of some of his works, such as the Biopik (1992), and in other works that have lethal potential such as Bed (1990), with its built-in mechanism for strangulation sex. Similarly, his caravans and campers do not merely express a utopian optimism, they display a desire for autonomy that is much more primitive, alluding to the vogue for survivalism, with all its fascistic overtones. Above all, the sculptures, tools, pieces of furniture and built structures that van Lieshout makes are direct and impulsive manifestations of a desire to create extensions of his own body.

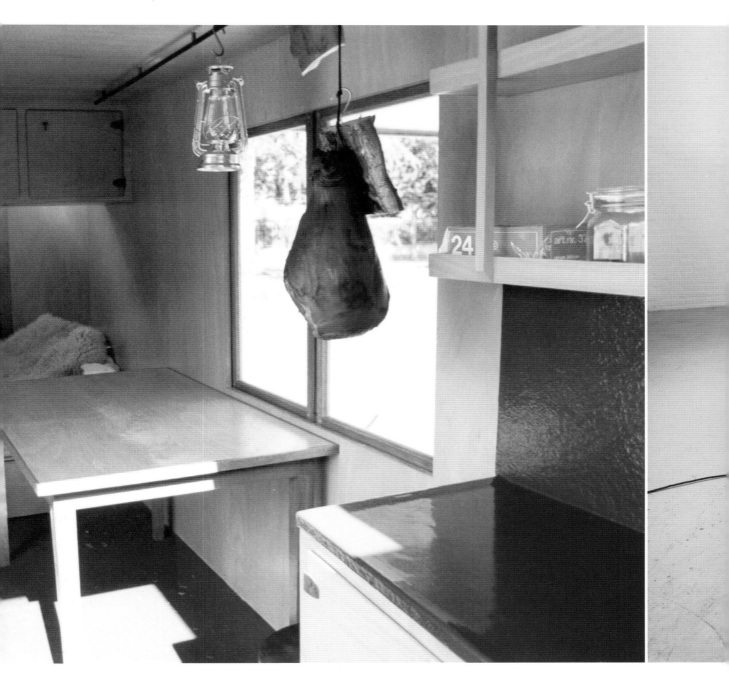

Orgone/Study/Book Skull, Sensory Deprivation Chamber (1997)

'The Good, The Bad and The Ugly'
Walker Art Center, Minneapolis (1998)
Interior view of wooden house attic

'The Good, The Bad and The Ugly'
Walker Art Center, Minneapolis (1998)
Exterior view

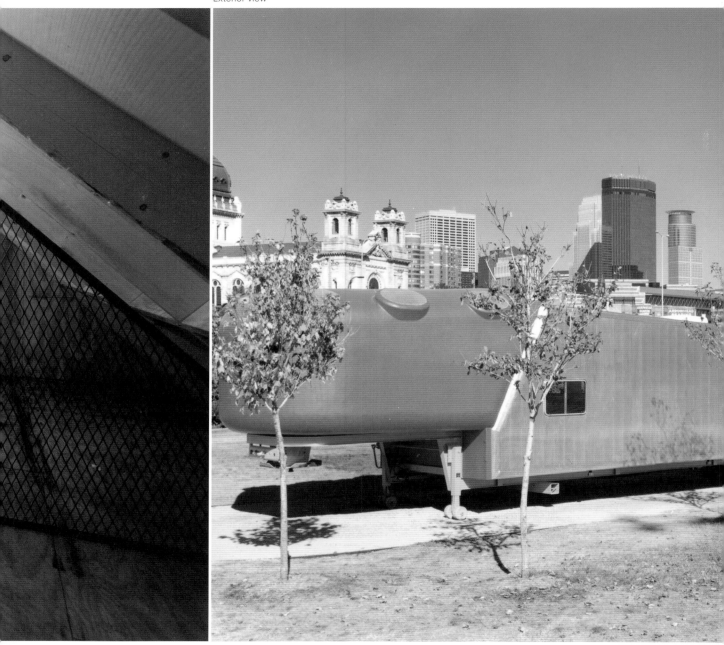

Faculty of Economics and Management Building, Utrecht
Bamboo garden

MECANOO

Faculty of Economics and Management Building, Utrecht
Second-floor plan

Faculty of Economics and Management Building, Utrecht
Aerial view

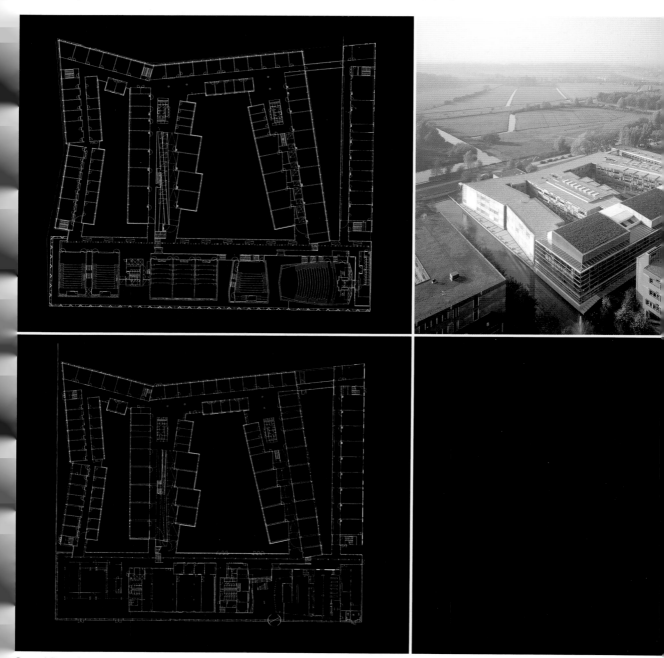

Ground-floor plan

Mecanoo is a typical Dutch representative of postmodernism. This may not be immediately obvious because the idiom of the studio's architecture is a modern one. But Mecanoo excels in quotations from modern and contemporary architecture, which are deployed in a variety of ways and manifest themselves in sophisticated, clear, efficient ground plans or in the atmosphere evoked by the design. Above all, Mecanoo's use of the vocabulary and methods of modern architecture reveals a confidence in the emancipatory power of that style, a faith that modern architecture is capable of shaping a better world. The quotations made their first appearance in the housing construction projects of the 1980s, which, with Mecanoo's clever typological variations and the close attention paid to designing the public spaces, set new standards in the Netherlands. The studio drew attention as one the first of many young architecture firms to carry out a major building, the student housing complex at Kruisplein (1985), Rotterdam. The architects won the competition for this project before they had even graduated, when the oldest member of the group was only just twenty-five. It seems to have set a trend in which more and more often clients entrusted their projects to young architects, a trend that reached a peak during the early 1990s.

The private residence that Francine Houben built (1989–91) in collaboration with Erick van Egeraat by the Kralingse Plas in Rotterdam impressively demonstrates the firm's capacities. A stone's throw from the famous Van Der Leeuw House by Brinkman and Van der Vlugt of 1929, it makes excellent use of its location, with the north side offering a prospect of the Kralingse Plas and the south side facing a small canal. An enclosed, Japanese-style garden is also located on the south side. Various living areas are linked by an atrium, which gives the house an open, transparent aspect, but which also succeeds in being relaxed and intimate.

Mecanoo built the Faculty of Economics and Management building (1995) on the Uithof site in Utrecht within a master plan prepared by OMA. The master plan prescribed a deep kasbah-like typology of up to three stories high, intended to keep the scheme as compact as possible and to spare the surrounding countryside. The existing tower blocks of the university faculties on the site would soar above the new buildings. In Mecanoo's project, the most public areas, such as the entrance lobby, lecture halls and canteen, are grouped on the north side facing the street, just behind a glazed façade. Separated by internal streets, this row of facilities forms a backbone along which four wings branch out to the rear. Each wing has a distinctive character and are separated by courtyards that differ in form and theme: one courtyard is a Zen garden with gravel and rocks, surrounded by façades of slatted-wooden panels; the middle courtyard contains a bamboo garden with a galvanized-steel-grid floor at first-floor level and is enclosed by galvanized-steel-grid façades; the third courtyard is a water garden with elevation partly in glass and partly clad in metal louvres, the only one with a view of the external

Faculty of Economics and Management Building, Utrecht
Stairwell in one of the buildings

Faculty of Economics and Management Building, Utrecht
Working space overlooking water garden and polder landscape

Faculty of Economics and Management Building, Utrecht
Restaurant

landscape. The buildings themselves differ in the type of access provided (either staircases or sloping ramps), in the materials used, in the way light is admitted and in the ground plan, which is articulated differently for each building. The individual rooms, lecture halls and laboratories all enjoy a view of one of the gardens and are grouped round a central access space that also functions as a meeting place. Offices vary in that they are located in the volume linking the other buildings at the rear, and these accommodations enjoy a view of the charming polder landscape to the south. The result is a differentiated building in which every space has a different atmosphere that the visitor can explore at leisure.

The new main library of Delft University of Technology (1997) is sited immediately behind the assembly hall built by van den Broek and Bakema in the 1960s. The older building, a brusque piece of concrete brutalism, is not a building that readily tolerates a close neighbour. Mecanoo solved this problem with a design that hardly looks like a building from the outside: by folding the ground plane upwards at an angle, the design produced something more like a sloping grassy hillock. The volume under the slanting slab accommodates the library, while an assembly hall retains a feeling of open space around it. The grass turf on the library roof is designed so that the students can sit outside on it in fine weather, which is also true of the steps of the gently inclined staircase that continues into the library interior and acts as a kind of sheltered public square. The only element that projects above the grass plane is a white cone, on top of the building like a beacon, particularly when it is spotlit at night. The library's glass walls have inflections here and there, with the result that they enter into a subtle visual poetry with the bluff forms of the library. The interior consists of a gigantic hall rising almost to the full height of the building, creating an extremely open – indeed, empty – impression despite being furnished with long tables. The surrounding walls are transparent, either because they are made of glass or because they are layered in design, with galleries offering access to offices, book stacks and floors with computer terminals. Storage of most of the books in the central repository underneath the hall made the atmosphere of transparency and emptiness possible. A spectacular feature, the glass-roofed cone, penetrates the roof, descends into the hall but remains floating just above the floor, allowing daylight deep inside the building.

Faculty of Economics and Management Building, Utrecht
Zen garden

Faculty of Economics and Management Building, Utrecht
Water garden

Houben House and Studio, Rotterdam
Exploded axonometric

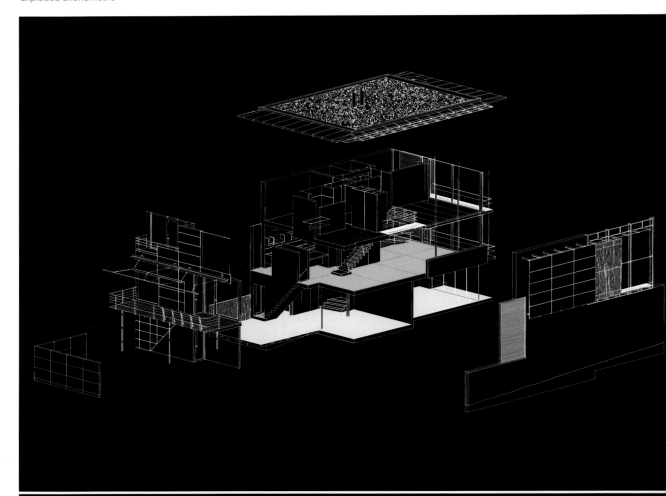

Houben House and Studio, Rotterdam
Front façade at night

Houben House and Studio, Rotterdam
Garden view

Houben House and Studio, Rotterdam
Library

Library, University of Technology, Delft
Plan

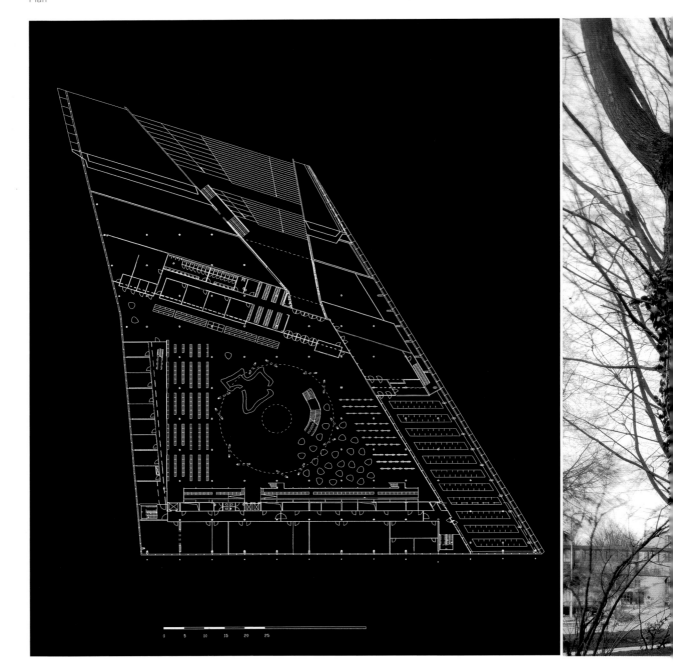

Library, University of Technology, Delft
Side view with auditorium by Bakema in background

Library, University of Technology, Delft
Entrance and roof garden

Library, University of Technology, Delft
Access to the cone and book stacks

Library, University of Technology, Delft
Study areas in the cone

Library, University of Technology, Delft
Lobby

Villa VPRO, Hilversum
Front façade with parking space and entrance

121

MVRDV

Villa VPRO, Hilversum
Night view

Villa VPRO, Hilversum
Side elevation

An abbreviation of the names of the three founders of the firm, Winy Maas, Jacob van Rijs and Nathalie de Vries, MVRDV is the architectural firm that best expresses the changes in Dutch society during the 1990s. The practice's proposals for planning and architectural projects have repeatedly confronted clients, users and viewers with new points of departure, exploring the tensions between laws and regulations on the one hand and the increase in individualization, deregulation and market forces on the other. The divergent interests of the parties involved in a building, the laws and regulations and above all the individuality of the occupiers and users are brought sharply into relief in each project, exposing the layers that comprise the eventual design. MVRDV displays the maximum spatial implications of each layer in a 'datascape', an updated version of what was formerly called a design's situation and planning envelope, which clarifies the optimal solutions. In the design process, the differences and conflicts between all these datascapes is negotiated as far as possible with each party until the point is reached where the design can be realized. It is, however, never smoothed over or reduced to a synthesis in the design. This stark stance gives the buildings an impudent, pragmatic and slightly anarchistic feeling, which becomes clearer once they start to be used.

MVRDV achieved their first success on winning the European competition with a design for housing called Berlin Voids. Although the design was never built, it immediately set the tone for their work. MVRDV concentrated all the homes in a single large block, so that a public space was created in the form of a void. Inside the block were no less than thirty-four different types of dwelling, distinctly visible from the outside due to the glass façade.

On a small scale, as a prototype for such a housing project, MVRDV, in partnership with Bjarne Mastenbroek, created twin houses in Utrecht, Villa KBWW (1997), in which an extensive experiment was carried out to gauge, through negotiations with prospective occupants and the authorities, how extremely divergent wishes could be accommodated within the available planning envelope.

In the one hundred WoZoCo (an acronym for the Dutch words Woon, Zorg and Complex, roughly translated as a sheltered housing development) units (1997) in Osdorp, west Amsterdam, individual dwellings are again notable for the variety of fenestration, doors and balconies on the rear of the building, but especially in the units that project from the front façade, a way of circumventing the constraints set out in the masterplan by van Eesteren. The dwellings are for people over the age of fifty-five, testifying to the fact that domestic architecture is increasingly catering to more specific target groups.

The offices of the VPRO broadcasting company (1997) in Hilversum is probably the best example of MVRDV's design method. The VPRO is a kind of collective public broadcasting company that has always held a special place in the Dutch media

Villa VPRO, Hilversum
Office landscape on 'giant staircase'

Villa VPRO, Hilversum
Interior patio

Villa VPRO, Hilversum
Interior with folded surface of executive car park

world. Transmission times are shared according to the number of members that the stations have acquired – comparable with the way political parties hold seats in parliament. The increased number of commercial channels in Holland in recent years has put considerable pressure on the public broadcasting system. The VPRO decided to leave its former accommodation, scattered throughout thirteen villas in Hilversum, and to house its staff in a single building to facilitate internal contact. Buildings for other broadcasting companies will eventually be built around the VPRO building, some of which are to be designed by MVRDV. The site is on the edge of woodlands and a heath, near a small lake.

MVRDV's solution is for a compact five-storey building that intrudes on the countryside as little as possible, even restoring a piece of nature in the form of a roof garden. In the interior every association with a typical office is avoided. There are no endless corridors with tiny rooms; the building opens up as a continuous extension of the landscape, where various office layouts can be implemented. All the floors are linked by ramps and 'superstairways', which have been designed so that they can double as seats during special events. The building's unusual form was made possible by negotiating the requirements for interior working conditions, light admission and exterior views with the future users.

With this background new variations were systematically introduced into the building, similar to how a city master plan is supported by an infrastructure and filled in with individual buildings. The space created is thus ready to be colonized by mini-buildings with private offices, improvised cells for concentrated work, with curtains and screens for privacy. In between are niches that can be claimed by nonconformists. Right from the start, it was felt that some of the furniture from the old villas should be rehoused along with the staff because it formed such a part of the identity of the individual editorial groups and programme teams. MVRDV has devised a supplementary programme for purchasing furniture, that again aims at creating differentiation. It is precisely this chaotic linking of different pieces and their associations that ensures that the VPRO office building is an unmistakable statement of the company's progressive and experimental identity, which has made it so immediately recognizable.

In the Dutch pavilion for Expo 2000 in Hanover, MVRDV's ideas are once more summed up like a manifesto. Instead of using the entire available terrain, a small tower was built as a stack of artificial landscapes, or 'ecologies', starting with a hilly landscape, going by way of a real wood (with the pots for the trees providing an intriguing space on the floor below) and an exhibition hall, to a pond on the roof where the rain water needed for irrigating the floors below is stored. The whole is a series of specific spaces that can be filled in thematically but allow the open space around the building to be free for temporary exhibitions, events and perhaps even for a little 'countryside'. Ideally, there would be windmills on the roof to provide the building's energy.

Villa VPRO, Hilversum
Entrance with folded surface and baroque lantern

The studio's installation 'Metacity/Datatown' (1999) demonstrates how the use of databases can be applied in political decision-making with regard to planning issues. Four computer-generated landscapes are projected onto a transparent cube in real time. Seen from the inside, data forms create an unbroken environment. With the assumption that certain regions throughout the world will develop into extended urban fields, or 'megacities', MVRDV conceived the hypothetical 'Datatown', a self-running city of 400 x 400 kilometres and a density of nearly 1500 inhabitants per square kilometre – about four times that of Holland. A number of 'what if' scenarios are let loose on this city to consider the implications for the urban environment. For instance, what would happen if all the residents of Datatown want to live in detached houses, or a structure of urban blocks, as preferred in Barcelona. What would happen if waste was dealt with in a different way or if we were all to become vegetarian? A total of fourteen of these virtual cities or scenarios were developed, which change as the visitor walks through them. In fact, Metacity/Datatown is based on the standard Dutch practice in which cultural bodies and city master plans do not propose schemes intended to be implemented as such, but to provoke a response in the political arena. Datatown is both a game and a serious study, an educational aid and a political instrument.

Villa VPRO, Hilversum
Floor plans

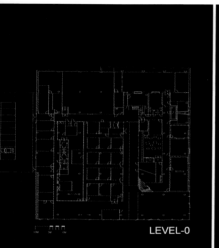

LEVEL-0

LEVEL-1

LEVEL-2

Villa VPRO, Hilversum
Radio studio

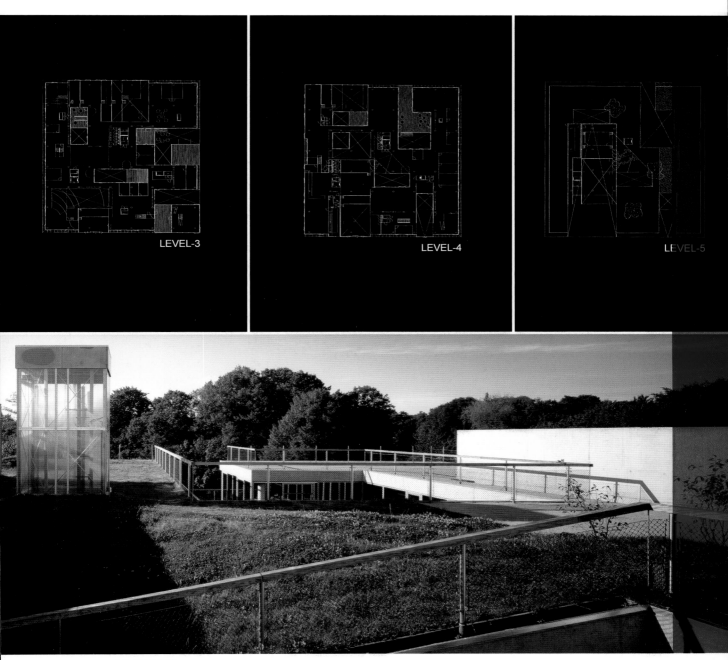

LEVEL-3

LEVEL-4

LEVEL-5

Villa VPRO, Hilversum
Roof garden

Villa KBWW, Utrecht
(in collaboration with Bjarne Mastenbroek)
View from park

161094
2 STOREYS 14M DEEP

231194
4 STOREYS 7 METER DEEP
NO WIDE VIEWS TO PARK

141294
HOUSE IN A HOUSE
NO ROOF ACCES HOUSE 1
SMALL GARDEN ACCES HOUSE 2

231295
ALTERNATING FLOORS 1
NO ROOF ACCESS FOR HOUSE 1

040195
ALTERNATING FLOORS 2
TO LITTLE GARDEN ACCESS FOR HOUSE 1

120195
ALTERNATING FLOORS 3
TO LITTLE GARDEN ACCESS FOR HOUSE 1

200295
ALTERNATING FLOORS 4
INCLUDES GARDEN ACCESS + ROOF ACCESS

090395
OUTDOOR SPACE
ROOFTERRACE HOUSE 1
GARAGE + ROOFTERRACE HOUSE 2

130495
FINAL RESULT
BEDROOMS IN 1+2
PIANOBLE HOUSE 2
INCL. FIRE REGULATIONS

Villa KBWW, Utrecht
Negotiation process showing integration of the two family units

Villa KBWW, Utrecht
Plans

Villa KBWW, Utrecht
Interior

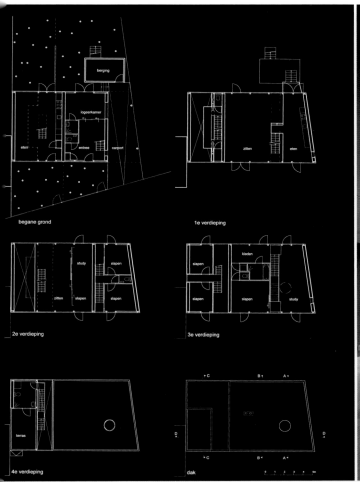

begane grond

1e verdieping

2e verdieping

3e verdieping

4e verdieping

dak

WoZoCo's, Amsterdam
Street façade

WoZoCo's, Amsterdam
Rear façade

WoZoCo's, Amsterdam
Site plan

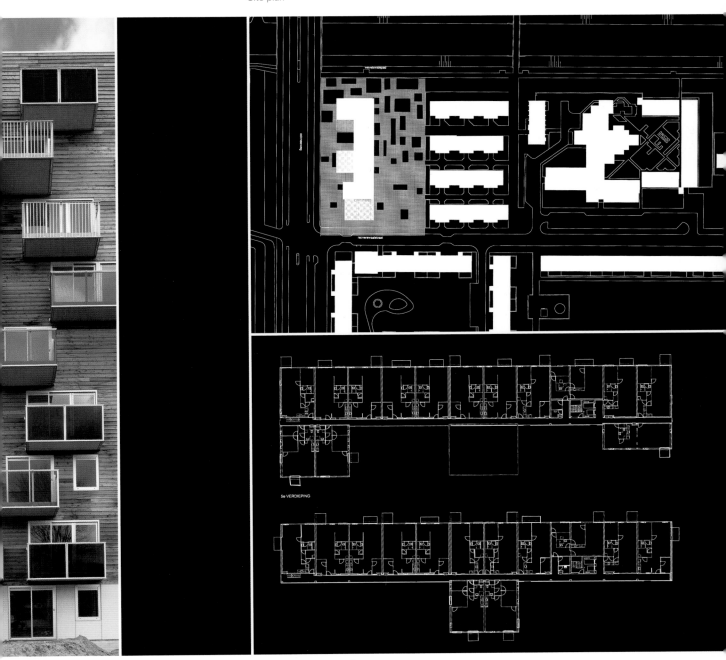

Fourth- and fifth-floor plans

WoZoCo's, Amsterdam
Cantilevered apartments

WoZoCo's, Amsterdam
External corridor

Metacity/Datatown
Installation view with video projection of exisiting megacities
São Paulo and Mexico City

Metacity/Datatown
Installation view

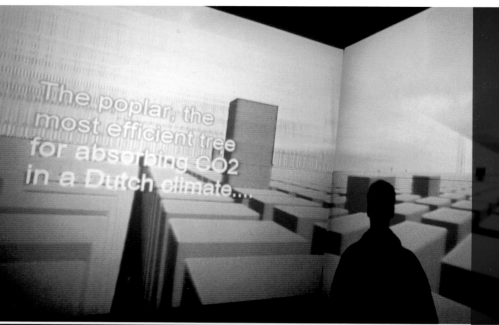

Dutch Pavilion, EXPO 2000, Hanover
Exterior view

Dutch Pavilion, EXPO 2000, Hanover
Aerial view

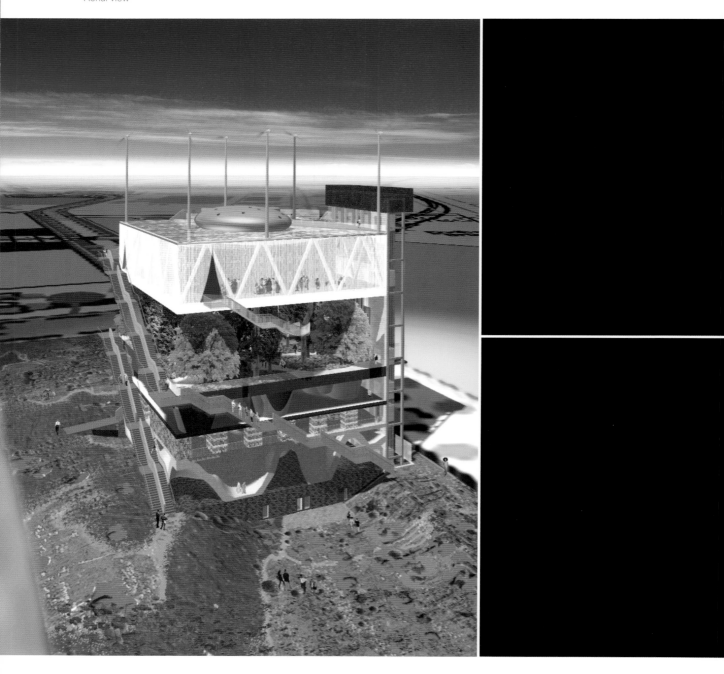

Dutch Pavilion, EXPO 2000, Hanover
Interior views

Minnaert Building, Utrecht
Front façade

145
|

NEUTELINGS
RIEDIJK

Minnaert Building, Utrecht
Entrance and bicycle storage

Minnaert building, Utrecht
Ground-floor plan

It was clear that Neutelings Riedijk was engaged in developing an idiosyncratic body of work right from the start from the intriguing cartoons Willem Jan Neutelings used in presenting his plans. Executed in clear, simple lines and inspired above all by Belgian cartoonists, the drawings set forth his design principles and generated an unmistakable aesthetic all their own.

Initially this aesthetic drew heavily on the modern architecture of the 1950s, such as that which one finds in the work of Dutch draughtsman and film-maker Joost Swarte, and was combined with a decorative use of materials covering large areas. In recent years, however, with his partner Michel Riedijk, Neutelings has distanced himself from an easily identifiable jargon. More than ever, the outward appearance of Neutelings Riedijk buildings conceals a precise and laconic elucidation of the forces that determine our built environment. This was first apparent in Neutelings's studies of the 'Ring Culture', the planning principles of the outskirts of Antwerp; the 'Carpet Metropolis', as it has developed between The Hague and Rotterdam; and the principles concerning the measurements of structures for different types of buildings. Beyond revealing a great interest in the anonymous laws that govern the built environment, these projects showed a preoccupation with mobilizing these laws to create an architecture and urban design that is flexible and diverse.

Today Neutelings Riedijk's research focuses on the rules and regulations as they are specified in the programme of building requirements. In larger commissions these laws specify 66 per cent of what the measurements of the spaces should be, what interior climate must prevail and even how the furniture is to be arranged. The remaining 34 per cent is not prescribed and is therefore the last bastion of freedom for an architect.

In such recent buildings as the Minnaert building (1997) on the Uithof in Utrecht and Veenman Printers (1997) in Ede, this space is concentrated at a single point in the middle of the building so as to present the people that use the building a specific architectural experience. In the case of Veenman Printers, this common area is the patio designed by West 8, onto which all the rooms look and that links the offices, consulting rooms and printshop itself.

The Minnaert building offers shared facilities – lecture halls, laboratories, offices and a restaurant – for the faculties of physics and astronomy, earth sciences, mathematics and information studies at the University of Utrecht and is linked with these faculty buildings by overhead walkways. All the common spaces are built as compactly as possible around an enormous central hall, with Moorish-style benches around the edge. Concentrating requirement-free space in the central hall, it became possible to let it be cold in the winter and warm in the summer and when it rains, the water flows towards large funnels in the roof and splashes down to the hall's slanting floor. There it forms a pool that ebbs and flows according to the season.

Minnaert Building, Utrecht
Conceptual drawings

Minnaert Building, Utrecht
Meeting alcoves in the lobby

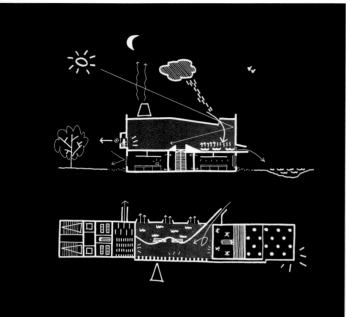

When the sun shines, beams of light enter through the same funnels. The studio aims to stimulate the senses with a changing interior climate in order to avoid the monotony of a standard building.

But the hall in the Minnaert building has another function. The rigid Dutch requirements for isolation have produced a paradoxical situation in which buildings hardly need any more heating, demanding instead permanent cooling, since the heat of lamps, people and computers no longer has any release. In the Minnaert building this heat is conveyed via chilled ceilings to a rain-water buffer, meaning that the temperature of the collected water rises each day by two degrees Celsius. At night this water is once more brought back to the roof, freely giving its warmth to the cold heavens.

Neutelings Riedijk state in no uncertain terms that their buildings are 'born naked' and that it is only once the concept is ready that the question of how they are to be clothed is addressed. The Minnaert building has been given a curiously pleated jacket in red clay tints; Veenman Printers has a transparent front that envelops the whole building, upon which every year new graphic designers can implement a design, although the present design by Karel Martens, based on a poem by K. Schippers, is likely to remain for a number of years. In the manner of cartoon captions, letters used as structural columns in the façade often inform the visitor of the name and function of Neutelings Riedijk buildings.

In the façade of the fire station (1999) in Maastricht, the architects allude to the meaning of the building in another way. The front façade's dark green panels are given a relief pattern that makes them appear as though they have been run over by a heavy lorry, alluding not only to the mighty fire engines that are the essence of the fire service but also to the site, characterized by major roads, railways and industrial complexes. The garage, two storeys high, is the undisputed centre of the building. To the rear are the ground-floor workshops, on the first floor the bedrooms; the second floor contains the offices, recreational areas and canteen. Over the garage on the second floor is a huge pool of the water used for extinguishing fires. Concealed behind the tough façade, it serves as a pond – with the spacious surrounding terrace, the water forms an unexpected oasis in the midst of noisy traffic and industry.

Although Veenman Printers still possesses a certain light-footed modernist elegance, the Minnaert building and the fire station are unfashionably strong in character, a quality of great importance to the architects. They are proud that they can persuade clients that it is often unnecessary for a new building to be plonked down in compliance with the latest trend. There are cases where they have opted instead for recycling existing buildings, as in the case of the Belgian Post Office, which wanted to build a new branch in Scherpenheuvel. Neutelings Riedijk proposed refashioning the existing villa and converted it to

accommodate counters and a canteen, while adding a kind of concrete bunker where mail can be sorted, money vans emptied and service bikes parked.

Minnaert Building, Utrecht
Restaurant

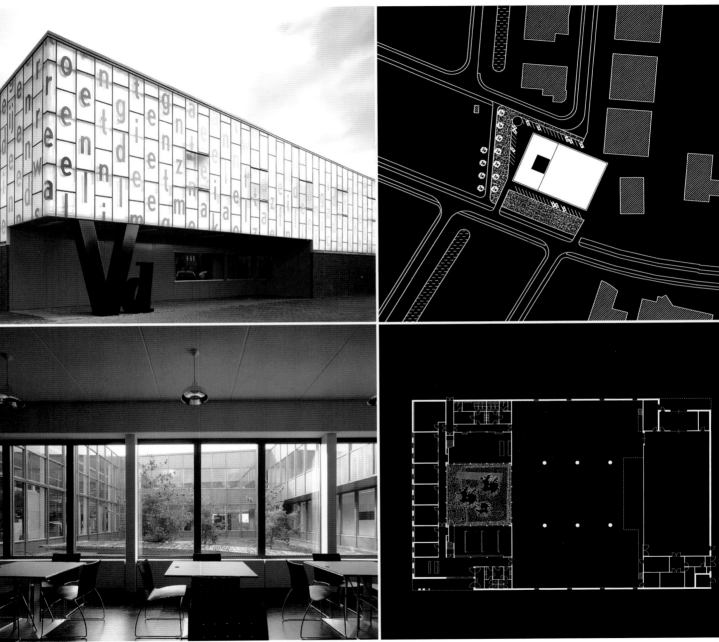

Veenman Printers, Ede
Main entrance

Veenman Printers, Ede
Site plan

Veenman Printers, Ede
View of the interior court from the restaurant

Ground-floor plan

Veenman Printers, Ede
View from the street

Post Office, Scherpenheuvel (Belgium)
Site plan

Plan

Post office, Scherpenheuvel (Belgium)
View by day

Fire Station, Maastricht
Night view of garage

Fire Station, Maastricht
Front (garage) façade

Fire Station, Maastricht

Fire Station, Maastricht
Garage interior

Site plan

Ground floor

First floor

Second floor

Fire Station, Maastricht
Interior view at upper level

Fire Station, Maastricht
Rooftop reservior

H₂O eXPO, Neeltje Jans
The well and interior

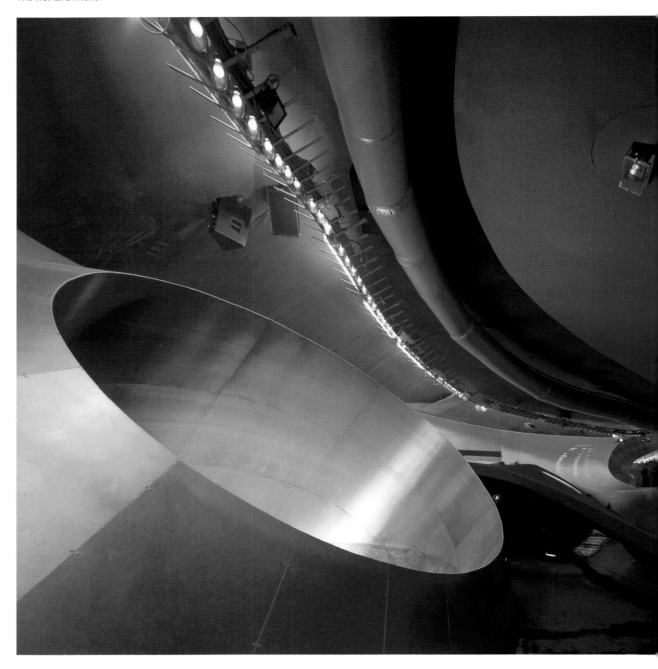

NOX

A practice that works with various media simultaneously, the Rotterdam-based studio NOX is not an architecture firm in the conventional sense. Originally established by Lars Spuybroek and Maurice Nio (the latter has since left), NOX produces videos, essays, books, magazines, websites and multimedia installations. *NOX Magazine*, which they published annually from 1991 to 1994, is an attractively designed series of publications in which writers and image-makers were invited to tackle certain themes. The nature and treatment of the themes – 'Actiones in Distans', 'Biotech', 'Chloroform' and 'Djihad' – was typical of NOX. Difficult subjects to confront, like black holes in the universe of information that we face daily, they were meant to draw us into reflection and speculation. The thread connecting the themes was the relation between modernity and technology, where the latter is not seen as something which is at the service of mankind, but as a complex configuration that has gradually smothered us entirely and now leads a life of its own.

Given this attitude towards technology, the thinking at NOX holds that it makes no sense to be confined within the limits of a single discipline. The architectural experience consists of a multiplicity of simultaneous sensory impressions. Not only are the dividing lines between the built environment and the realm of media becoming ever more vague, but the distinction between direct physical action and 'remote control' is similarly fading. NOX is fascinated by these developments but takes a critical stance, making use of every technique and technology the electronic age has to offer, sometimes in combination with mechanical technologies, both in the design process and in the final product. But always NOX adds an unexpected twist. The perceptual fuses with the conceptual in NOX's work; there is no beginning or end and everything is in a continual state of flux. This fluidity constitutes a perpetual 'in-between' on which the designers 'surf' and where the users or inhabitants are continually challenged to take an active role.

Lars Spuybroek sees the computer primarily as an instrument that will effect a revolution comparable to the discovery of perspective in the Renaissance, an instrument that enables us to visualize the real world in a different way, including aspects of that world that are imperceptible to the naked eye. Since all information is converted into flows of data, things of the most diverse nature can be brought into relation. But, like perspective, the computer is also a design instrument by which a plan can be mapped onto the world – literally, as a projection, and figuratively, in the sense of an architectural project.

It is no longer necessary for a NOX project to manifest itself by traditional means, which liberates architecture to control and influence all possible systems. For example, a recent competition design for a 'tower' in Doetinchem, which NOX

H$_2$O eXPO, Neeltje Jans
Exterior and entrance

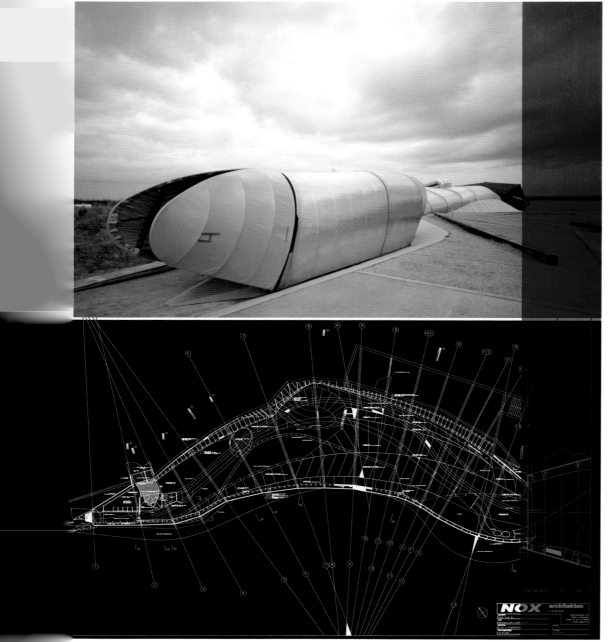

H$_2$O eXPO, Neeltje Jans
Plan

produced together with the artist Q. S. Serafijn, is conceived as an interactive website where a virtual form (the tower) materializes above the city in reaction to such variables as electricity consumption or telephone activity in certain neighbourhoods, patterns of material consumption; or information provided by the inhabitants themselves. All the data is compiled and represented in twelve three-dimensional maps above the normal city street plan, allowing inhabitants to check what is happening at their home address whenever they like. To some extent they can influence that situation by changing their behaviour or by entering new information. Each of the twelve maps has its own centre of gravity, which is continually recalculated and thus constantly changes position over the city. The combined centre of gravity, which becomes the apex of the 'tower', migrates above the city accordingly. The residents of the plot above which the apex of the tower is located on 31 December of each year receive a prize of 10,000 Euros. The project can be followed on the Internet, but there is also a house one can visit. The overall result is an improbable composite of art, architecture, urban planning, new media and TV game-show.

Each of the five senses are activated in one of NOX's buildings – visually, aurally, and through smells, temperatures and tastes. The most important sense that Lars Spuybroek addresses, however, is that of proprioception, the body's sense of disposition and movement. In this respect, the work of NOX may be understood as attempting to avoid the grim picture of the future sketched by Paul Virilio in his book *L'Inertie Polaire*. Virilio predicts that the pervasiveness of new media in the future will turn people into pathetic, helpless couch potatoes. In order to stimulate the body, the floors in NOX's designs are rarely horizontal and merge seamlessly with the walls, as in the experimental architecture of Paul Virilio and Claude Parent in the 1960s. Spuybroek refers to his H_2O eXPO Pavilion (1994–97) as a 'rolled-up urban square'. Tables and chairs in NOX's designs move when you come into contact with them, as in the V2 Lab (1998), an experimental workshop for new media in Rotterdam. The electronics are similarly interactive, in some cases requiring the visitor to use physical force to obtain the desired effect.

The V2 Lab is part of the V2 Organization for Unstable Media in Rotterdam, a cultural institution that investigates the cultural and social consequences of electronic media. The V2 Lab itself is a laboratory in which artists and others can work on specific cultural projects for which they need media equipment and advice. NOX's design for the space involves the conversion of a former newspaper printing office into a multifunctional space for exhibitions and lectures, which are located on the ground floor. On the floor above is a media laboratory, consisting of booths with facilities for videomontage and postproduction and a larger, hilly 'landscape' with a meandering table on which people can work on computers in a space surrounded by a transparent

V2 Lab, Rotterdam
Reception

wall; the reception desk is part of a larger 'landscape' and the formal concept. The overall idea is based on the deformation of the existing building's orthogonal grid structure by means of animation software, and the introduction of a system of springs and strings within that system. Spuybroek writes, 'The concept is the result of a literal media criticism of architecture, because within a medium events progress by means of waves, not just within the topological continuity of the event itself, but more to induce movement within this continuity by passing on forces within the field. The Euclidian distinction between a line and a point prohibits this, as each point rather effectuates the separation of lines that stimulates their joining. By contrast, here this point constitutes a knot, capable of shrinking and expanding, scientifically known as a SPRING, a non-static point capable of passing on force.'

The H_2O pavilion is a permanent exhibition facility erected on Neeltje Jans, an artificial island made to aid construction of the Schelde flood barrier. NOX designed the pavilion dedicated to freshwater (the adjoining marine part was designed by Kas Oosterhuis; see pages 208–11). The form was generated on a computer using animation software and as such is a typical example of 'liquid architecture'. Unlike such designs by other architects, it is not simply the form of the building that is fluid. Inside, the visitor is confronted with the liquidity of water in countless ways: the water flows and boils, there is mist and condensation, and some parts of the walls are so cold that a layer of ice builds up. The interior also contains sound and light effects, including projections of the molecular structure of water and of wave patterns. Visitors activate these wave patterns by passing light-sensitive cells, touching sensors or operating handles.

The emphasis on physical experience recalls early projects by Coop Himmelb(l)au, such as 'Hard Space' and 'Soft Space' of 1970 or the 'Flammenflügel' of 1980. But NOX's H_2O eXPO Pavilion, with its curvaceous silver exterior and media-filled interior, is above all reminiscent of the Philips Pavilion at the Brussels World Exhibition of 1958 by Le Corbusier with Janis Xenakis. Le Corbusier asked Xenakis to design a pavilion because he wanted to make a building that was pure interior, a place for Edgad Vaèse to realize a spectacular production of sound and light that would address every physical sense. Xenakis, now known primarily as a composer, produced a piece of 'music' for the interval, in which the creaking sound of smouldering charcoal spread through the space over 365 loudspeakers, a sound that suggested the structure was under such stress that it was about to collapse. NOX's pavilion possesses a comparable integration of architecture and media, but they are so structurally integrated that one can scarcely speak of architecture or interior. Rather, it is an all-embracing situation, an event-space on the theme of 'wateriness', through which visitors must find their

V2 Lab, Rotterdam
Concept drawings

D-Tower
Media tower for the city of Doetinchem
(In collaboration with Q.S. Serafijn)

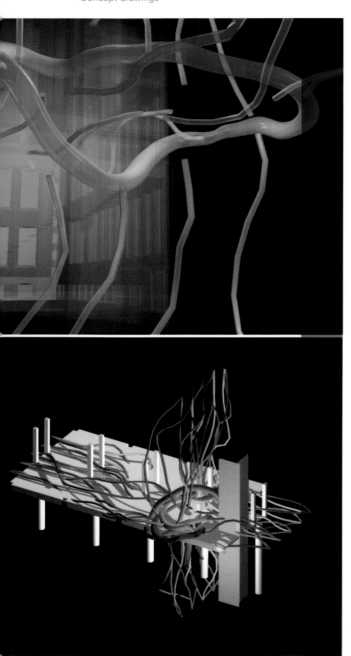

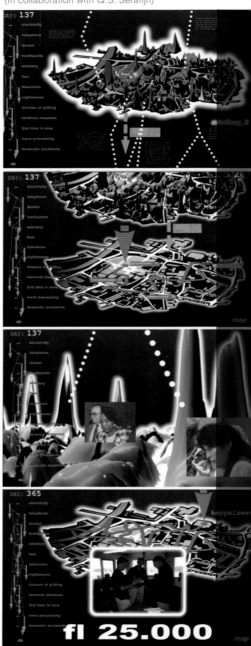

own way. The H$_2$O eXPO Pavilion is a multimedia tribute to the tradition of the 1960s and 1970s, when Marshall McLuhan saw ideal opportunities for people to learn to cope with the sensory bombardment of the new media.

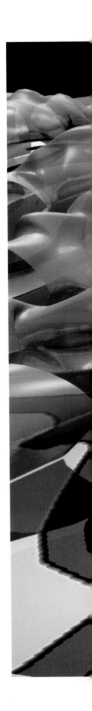

Off-the-road 5-speed
Housing quarter, Eindhoven
Overall view

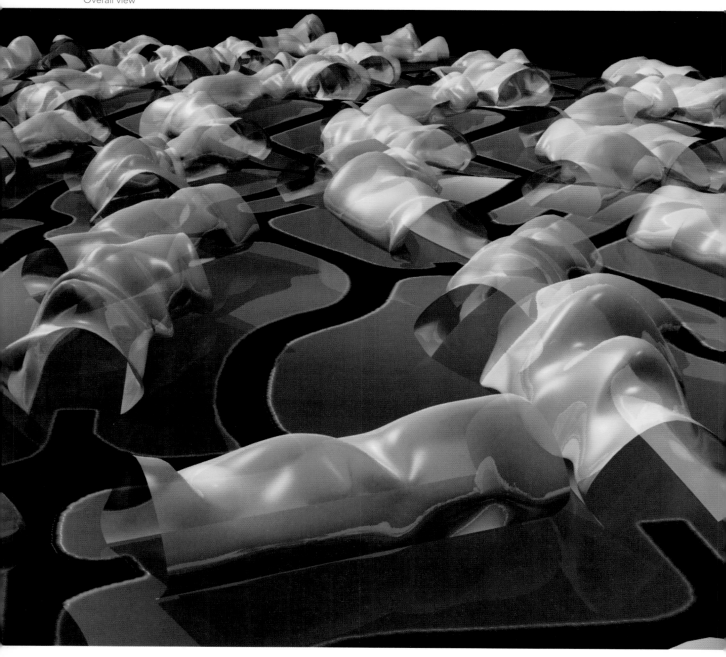

Off-the-road 5-speed
Double house

Off-the-road 5-speed
Single house

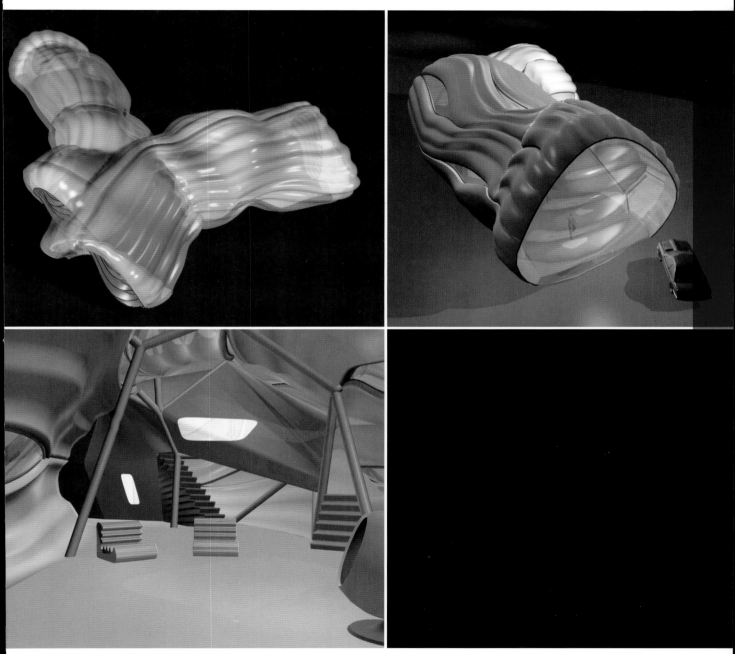

Off-the-road 5-speed
Interior

KunstHAL, Rotterdam
Street façade

OFFICE FOR METROPOLITAN ARCHITECTURE (OMA)

KunstHAL, Rotterdam
Ramp connecting park and street, main entrance

KunstHAL, Rotterdam
Auditorium

OMA occupies an exceptional position in the Dutch and international architecture landscapes. To assess the firm solely on the basis of its built work would be an injustice. OMA has, of course, produced buildings and major urban planning projects, but the firm is above all a laboratory that is continually trying to devise new solutions for the problems of a society marked by ever-increasing congestion and instability. In other words, much of OMA's work can be regarded as research. Much of this research takes place within the framework of design commissions and competitions in the form of experimental design or design experiments. However, it also includes independent studies, an important part of which are the publications of Rem Koolhaas: *Delirious New York* (1978); such essays as 'Bigness', 'Atlanta', 'Singapore Songlines' and 'The Generic City'; and what is, so far, his magnum opus, *S, M, L, XL* (1995). This last theoretical study is being continued in an intensified form by Koolhaas's Harvard Project on the City, which investigates topics like the rise of megacities in Asia and the influence of shopping on the city. All these projects scrutinize existing views and justifications of architecture. Indeed paradoxically, the entire oeuvre of Rem Koolhaas and OMA is marked by a radical scepticism towards the architectural profession as a design discipline. Through countless unexecuted projects and studies, OMA has attempted to come to grips with urban culture in a far more radical manner than the realization of incidental buildings. These projects have not infrequently introduced totally new typologies that precisely meet the needs of the second modernity.

A good example of an extremely influential unexecuted project is the design for a public library on the university campus in Jussieu, Paris (1993). Consisting of a multiply folded continuous floor surface that smoothly extends the public deck underneath existing buildings, it has no walls and the façade is only sketchily designed, which makes it possible to lay out each floor in a free and adaptable way.

OMA applied the same folded-floor principle to the Educatorium (1997), which provides a central facility shared by the faculties of the University of Utrecht, although the requirements of the brief made it necessary to abandon the total freedom of floor layout. Apart from two large lecture halls and examination rooms, it contains a 1000-seat cafeteria, restaurant for university staff and a cycle garage for 1000 bicycles. It is intended as a meeting place for the university's 30,000 staff and students, who are presently spread over a considerable number of buildings on a large site called De Uithof at the edge of the city. OMA also prepared the master plan for the campus, which encompasses numerous other interesting buildings including Neutelings' Minnaert building (pages 144–52), Mecanoo's Faculty of Economics and Management building (pages 104–09) and, in the future, a library by Wiel Arets and a laboratory by UN Studio.

The Educatorium's sloping floors bring about an entirely new kind of spatial experience in which it is hard to tell where the

KunstHAL, Rotterdam
Site plan

KunstHAL, Rotterdam
View from Museumpark

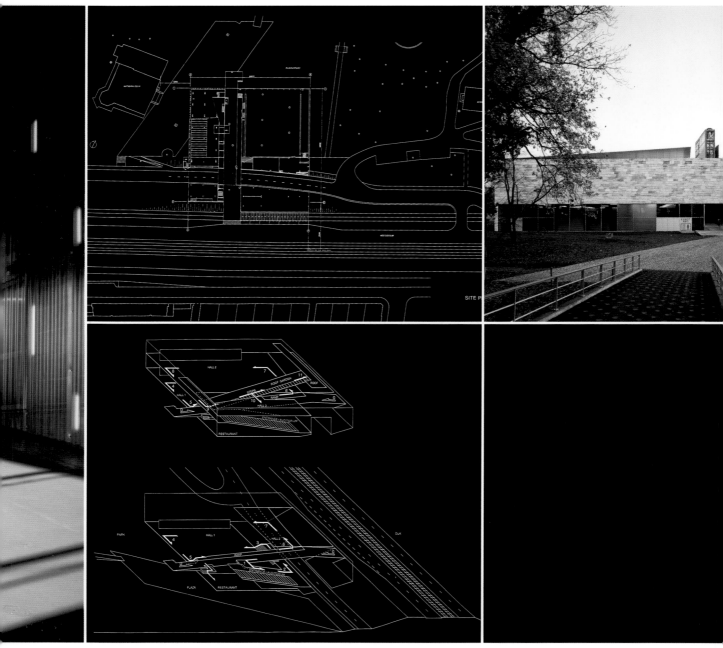

KunstHAL, Rotterdam
Axonometrics showing distribution
of spaces and circulation

exterior ends and the interior begins. Passing through doors without noticing the transition, one does not observe any staircases or even thresholds – visitors glide into the building. Once inside, movement is imperceptible from one level to another, even though staircases are here and there, where the vertical distance to be bridged is sufficient to warrant one. Some stairs rise gently as extensions of the sloping floors, as do those in and alongside the auditoriums, but others form monumental spaces in their own right. Roaming through, one has a feeling not unlike when exploring a virtual space on the computer, a sensation that there are alternative paths to your left, right, behind, in front and even above and below. And there are other bold gestures, such as a glass floor at an upper level, which confronts the user explicitly with its spatial structure, giving one a sensation of floating in space. Floors and corridor walls shine and reflect; they are either transparent or registered as surfaces by illumination. Materials and construction assume an explicit presence in the lecture halls and examination rooms.

The KunstHAL (1992) in Rotterdam was intended to continue in the city's festival tradition that arose out of necessity after the war. Containing art galleries, a large auditorium and restaurant, the building's ingenious form allows users to establish different routes and interspatial connections, and hence various connections between programmes. It is as though a box had been tied in a knot: the building is transected by a ramp that structures its routing and leads from the lower-level Museumpark (a public space also designed by OMA in collaboration with Yves Brunier) to the higher-level river dyke and across a road at the foot of the same dyke. All the larger spaces have glazed façades, except the exhibition rooms, whose interiors must be protected from direct daylight. The surrounding landscape is drawn into the interior of the building, a continuity that culminates in the roof garden. The façades feature natural stone facing the park and the road and crude concrete on the sides. A tower containing engineering services carries a billboard designed to draw the KunstHAL to the attention of highway motorists speeding by. The lower hall adjoining the park has columns made of tree trunks, while the auditorium can be made smaller by drawing a huge rolling curtain, which somewhat resembles a circus tent when fully extended.

The Congrexpo (1994) is a crucial building in the urban scheme OMA designed for Lille, France. Extension of the high-speed railway system from Paris to Brussels and London suddenly gave the sleepy provincial city a strategic position in Europe, on which OMA's plan intended to capitalize with a new commercial zone, adjacent to the existing historical centre, with shopping mall, offices, hotels and a new railway station. There is also a conference centre and exhibition hall. The pairing of these two functions means that the Congrexpo building could vary multiple combinations of the two; the main auditorium is large enough to stage rock concerts. It is a gigantic building and makes a big

Library, Jussieu (Paris)
Model (winning competition design)

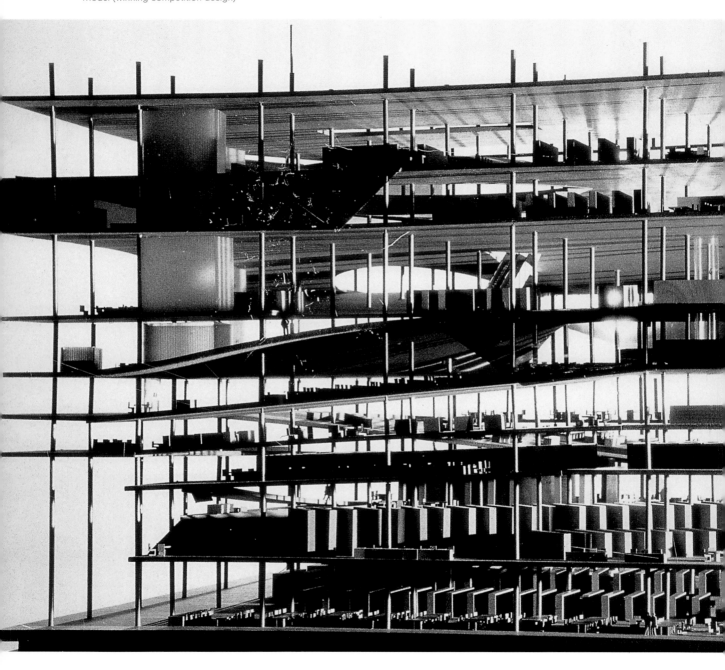

impression despite its fragmentary detailing. The finish is exceptionally brusque, a choice that is partly explained by the low budget and time constraints on the building project. Bars and toilets, raw and minimalist in design, were designed by Joep van Lieshout.

Like many of the architects from the heroic period of modern architecture in the 1920s and 1930s, OMA has experimented widely with dwelling typologies, which has applied not only to larger residential projects, such as the one designed for Fukuoka in 1991, but to a series of private house designs.

The Villa dall'Ava (1991) in Paris and the Villa Bordeaux (1998) make especially clear what OMA is after. In both houses, the living areas are left as free as possible to allow the occupants to change arrangements of furniture and curtains. The walls of these levels are completely transparent and can be slid partly or wholly open. The ground plan blends seamlessly into the landscape, as in the Villa dall'Ava, or offers an uninterrupted vista of the surroundings, as in the Bordeaux house, while the living level is sandwiched between two floors containing individual bedrooms, studies and other rooms, which are separated as much as possible. In the Villa dall'Ava, for example, a swimming pool was placed between the parents' bedroom and that of their daughter; there is a private study in the basement. The family is thus fragmented and individual members can regroup freely in the flexible space on the intermediate floor. Ingenious systems of staircases and ramps connect the individual rooms with the collective space.

The Bordeaux house features a room that moves up and down through the house like a lift. Primarily conceived to allow the disabled client to move easily throughout the house in a wheelchair, the solution went well with Koolhaas's fascination for the potential applications of lifts. He had already discovered the possibilities when he studied New York, but he gradually worked them out in more detail over a period of years, for example in the design of an addition to the Museum of Modern Art, New York (1998) and in the Hyperbuilding (1997). The structure of OMA's private houses makes them act as condensers, both literally, through the form and the force-field they exert, and figuratively, in the tradition of the social condensers of the Russian Constructivists.

Though small, the public toilet OMA designed in collaboration with the photographer Erwin Olaf, is as much a social condenser as the firm's other buildings. Sited on a spot that has long been a meeting place for gay men, opposite a café that puts tables out on the pavement during the summer, the structure consists of a men's and women's toilet separated by a shared wall of corrugated glass on which Olaf has provided an image depicting 'the battle of the sexes'. The design is meticulously detailed – a pavilion in the style of Philip Johnson's Glasshouse, with a toilet pan of stainless steel, a mosaic urinal and a roof in which large pieces of glass are embedded like jewels.

Rem Koolhaas occasionally expresses doubts about his own buildings because, despite their inventiveness, they could still be regarded as conventional architecture. But it is an intelligent architecture, responding sensitively to the programme and context and possessing a strength to instigate change, which holds true for buildings very large and very small.

Educatorium, Utrecht
Entrance with sculptures, benches and lights
by Atelier van Lieshout

Educatorium, Utrecht
Axonometrics of different levels

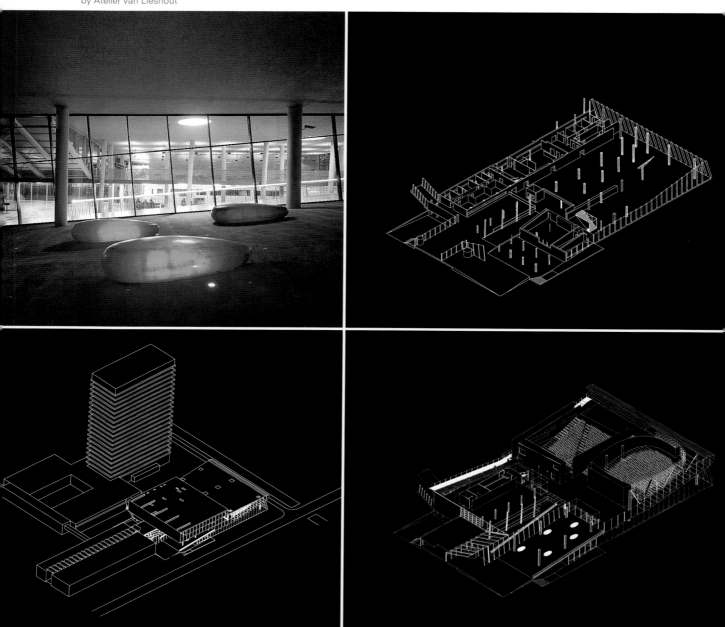

Educatorium, Utrecht
Axonometric

Educatorium, Utrecht
Restaurant

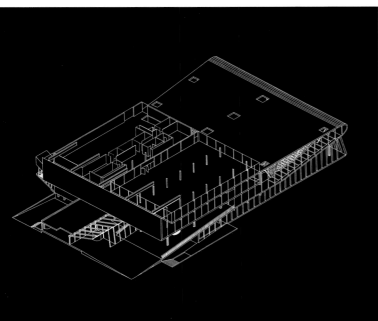

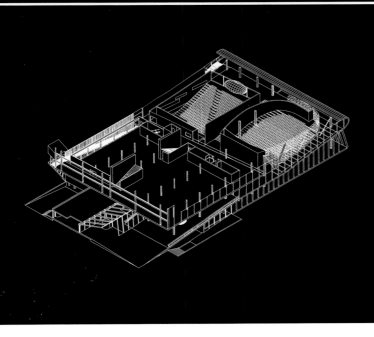

Educatorium, Utrecht
Lobby

Educatorium, Utrecht
Stairwell

Educatorium, Utrecht
Lobby of auditorium with projection cabin

Euralille, Lille (France)
Railway viaduct and tower by Christian Portzamparc

Euralille, Lille (France)
Shopping mall by Jean Nouvel

Euralille, Lille (France)
Masterplan

Congrexpo, Lille (France)
Sketches showing distribution of spaces: auditorium,
conference halls, exposition space and parking

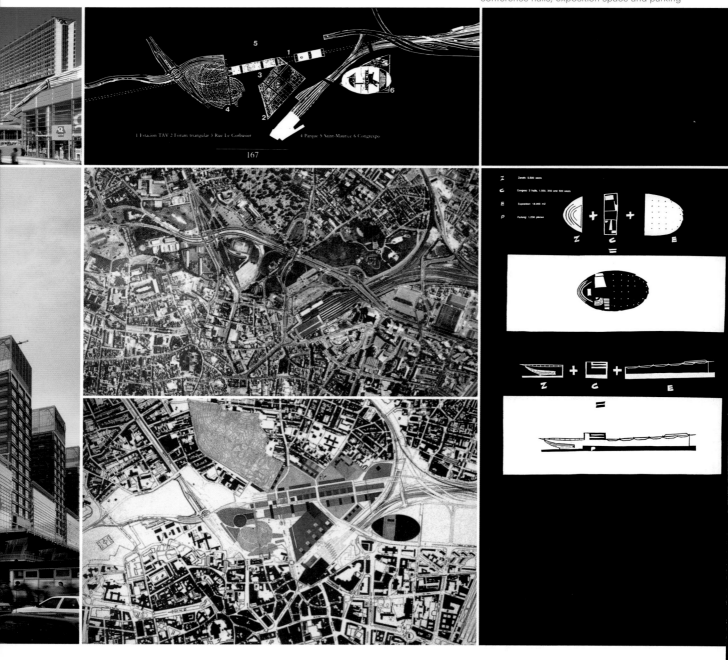

Congrexpo, Lille (France)
Exterior view

Congrexpo, Lille (France)
Exterior view

Congrexpo, Lille (France)
Contrasting façade treatments:
conference centre (left), exhibition hall (right)

Congrexpo, Lille (France)
Stairs to auditorium for popular music concerts

Congrexpo, Lille (France)
Exhibition hall

Congrexpo, Lille (France)
Corridor

Congrexpo, Lille (France)
Main hall of the conference centre

Congrexpo, Lille (France)
Staircase in conference centre

Villa Bordeaux
Exterior view

Villa Bordeaux
Patio

Villa Bordeaux
First-floor plan

Ground-floor plan

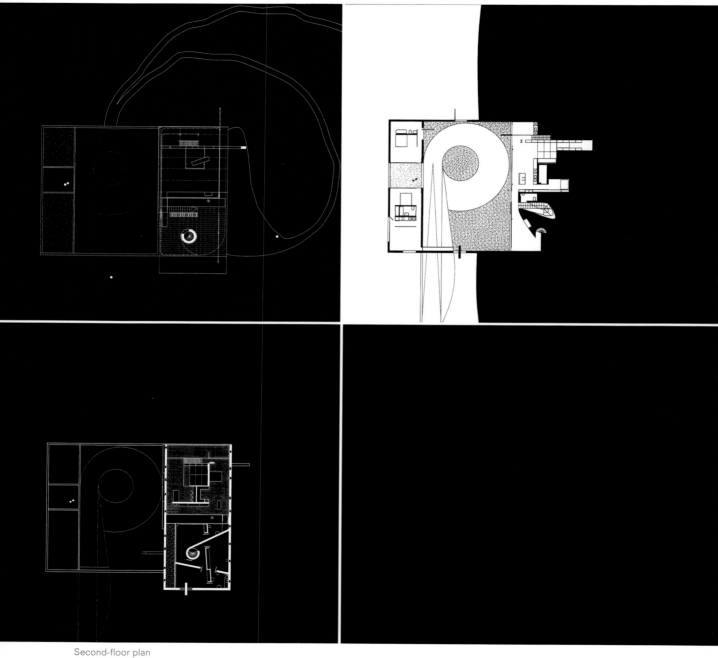

Second-floor plan

Villa Bordeaux
Exterior view

Villa Bordeaux
View of the elevating studio at the heart of the house

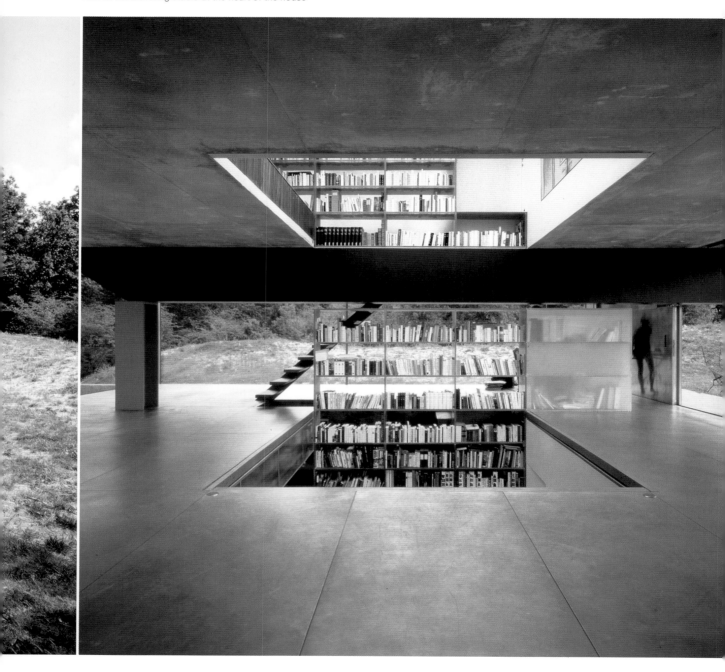

Villa Bordeaux
Detail of elevating studio

Villa Bordeaux
Window in lower bedroom

Villa Bordeaux
Kitchen

Villa Bordeaux
View in urban setting

Public Toilet, Groningen
Exterior

Public Toilet, Groningen
Detail

Garbage Transfer Station, Zenderen
Exterior view

OOSTERHUIS.NL

Garbage Transfer Station, Zenderen
View from street

Garbage Transfer Station, Zenderen
Aerial view

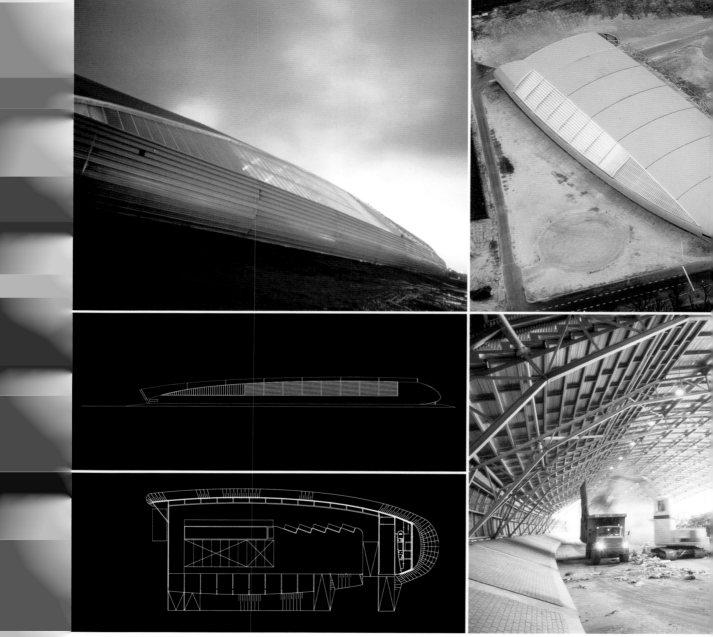

Garbage Transfer Station, Zenderen
Elevation and plan

Garbage Transfer Station, Zenderen
Interior view

The firm of Kas Oosterhuis, Oosterhuis.NL, is really no more a conventional architectural practice than NOX (page 163–74), although the dividing line between classic architectural design and new media applications is sometimes rather clearer than with NOX. Oosterhuis and his wife, the artist Ilona Lénard, took an early interest in the potential of the computer as a design tool and are regarded as pioneers in the area. They have have published extensively on the subject, frequently give lectures and lead workshops about it. Oosterhuis and Lénard started by using the mouse and screen as a direct, two-dimensional freehand sketching medium, but they later became interested in the computer's potential for designing three-dimensional freeforms. Almost invariably these forms are used to erect buildings that look sculptural from the outside – in some cases the building's shape is sculptural, in other cases the physical structure is partly disguised by a 'dazzle painting' and in yet others a combination of the two is used. Dazzle painting is a camouflage technique invented during World War II to make ships invisible to enemy submarines. In contrast to the exteriors, the interiors of Oosterhuis's buildings are usually rather businesslike – a simple filling-in of the structure to satisfy the requirements of the brief.

Oosterhuis and Lénard have continued to consider the future role of computers in architecture. They have, for example, been experimenting with the Internet as a medium for design workshops, in which a number of designers – or web surfers – work simultaneously on a single form from which three-dimensional models can be derived. They have also explored the use of computers for the fine control of interior environments in combination with winter gardens and horticultural greenhouses, as in the City Fruitful project. In Oosterhuis's design for the salt-water section of the H_2O eXPO Pavilion (1997, the freshwater part was designed by NOX, pages 164–67), the whole building was conceived as an organism that is connected to what happens inside and outside it, a node in space.

Oosterhuis questions the distinction between nature and culture. People visiting the salt-water part of the pavilion are assailed by veritable floods of water, and seem at certain moments to be walking through an artificial underwater world. Yet Oosterhuis writes, 'we no longer think of the "artificial" and the "natural" in antithetical terms. We regard the omnipresent artificial world, the global synthetic system, as one immense complex organism.' The behaviour of the pavilion is not controlled purely by preprogrammed algorithms, it reacts to visitors' movements and to fluctuations in the environment. A weather station continually monitors wind speed and water levels in the vicinity of the pavilion and transmits this data to a computer system, which then uses it to calculate an 'emotive factor', in turn influencing the systems that control sound and light within the pavilion. The building hosts a continual game of real and virtual environments, situations that merge seamlessly into one another, with the building extending into virtual space. The

saltwaterpavilion, Neeltje Jans
Exterior view

complexity of all that is happening is so great that the pavilion seems to be alive.

In a related way the Waste Distribution Centre (1995) in Zenderen is another good example of merging functions. Waste from the surrounding region is collected there before being transported to a temporary dump and incineration facility. The design is a gigantic composition of ellipsoids, an abstract blob uniting all the functions (office, waste handling and water purification) within it.

A project that plays with these themes in an urban context is paraSITE (1997–98), initially developed in Rotterdam, an inflatable sculpture whose interior contains computers that are linked to a website. Composers and artists at remote locations can use this setup to influence the behaviour of the paraSITE. Their contributions are combined into a collective production and rendered through loudspeakers, producing a remarkable effect somewhere between language and music. The computer software has a learning capacity so when it returns to Rotterdam after touring various cities an entirely different production will have evolved.

saltwaterpavilion, Neeltje Jans
Interior view

saltwaterpavilion, Neeltje Jans
Interior view

paraSITE, Rotterdam
Canal-side view

paraSITE, Rotterdam
Interior

Megacinema, Rotterdam
View from the Schouwburgplein (designed by West 8)

215

KOEN VAN VELSEN

Megacinema, Rotterdam
Façade detail

Megacinema, Rotterdam
Section

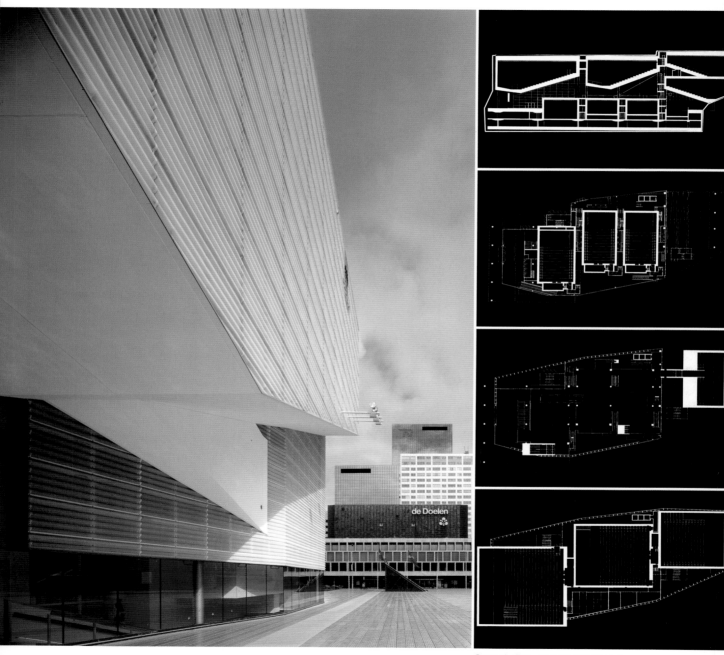

Ground-, first-, and second-floor plans

Koen van Velsen made a name for himself early on with a series of building alterations and extension projects, large and small, in which a discrete element was inserted into a historical context. The added elements were always light and transparent in character, and in most cases the use of modern materials produced a strong contrast. During the 1980s, van Velsen continued to develop his practice of detaching parts of his buildings until a point was reached when every component of his design had an autonomous character. In van Velsen's first masterwork, the public library in Zeewolde (1985–89), he took this approach to such an extreme that even the structure of the façade's different materials gives the appearance of a compilation of independent components. Although van Velsen has an aversion to theory, his 1980s project can perhaps best be characterized as an idiosyncratic, paradoxical synthesis of a typically Dutch structuralism, in the tradition of Aldo van Eyck and Herman Herzberger, yet lacking the associated moralistic aspects, deconstructivism, and the philosophical underpinnings associated with such work.

Much of this synthesis is evident in his design for the Rijksakademie (1985–92), Amsterdam, though in a rather more relaxed and pragmatic form. The project involved the conversion of the former Cavalry Barracks, built in 1863 and not far from the city centre. The Rijksakademie is a postgraduate art institute that does not give classes as such or follow a teaching programme: candidates for places must have completed art-school training and are expected to devise their own working plan to attract the interest of the academy's professors; their success in doing so determines whether their participation will extend beyond the first year. Van Velsen's first step was to represent the organization of the academy as a number of diagrams, a procedure he always follows. He explains his completed designs in much the same way: practically without words. The technical workshops are located on the ground floor of the barracks' hollow square block with the studios above them – all are contained within the original structure. A new block occupies the centre of the courtyard and contains the entrance vestibule, reception desk, library, slide library, offices, the *studium generale* department (which organizes various cultural activities), exhibition spaces, an auditorium and a photographic studio (which was too tall to fit into the old building). From this central volume access to the departments of painting, drawing, sculpture and graphics is via transparent footbridges. Wherever the footbridges enter the old building, a new departmental centre has been built containing a staircase and offices for department coordinators and staff. In two cases, the footbridges extend beyond the existing square block into small new volumes, one of which contains the restaurant, the other two large project studios. The new structure is superimposed on the old at an angle to the original axes, thereby explicitly declaring itself as a set of new, independent elements with a visual treatment distinct from that of the old building. Wherever possible, restoration work has been done on the old building, not in an overly meticulous way, which

Megacinema, Rotterdam
Lobby

would have clashed with the building's original function, but so that some of the historical fabric remains visible. In the attic, for example, the old grey paintwork has been preserved, including graffiti that the soldiers have scratched into it over the years. The new additions and alterations are exceptionally sober in character and are practically undesigned – white plasterwork, galvanized steel, glass, wood, concrete and pipe insulation are all left unconcealed – which gives the Rijksakademie a convincing, no-nonsense atmosphere in the tradition of the industrial lofts in which working artists so often make their studios.

The design of the multiplex cinema (1992–96) on Schouwburgplein in Rotterdam is intended to reinforce the function of the urban entertainment centre that already includes the Schouwburg theatre and the De Doelen concert hall. Extending the public square into the building, the foyers of the multiplex cinema are accessible to the public all day and contain cafés and restaurants. Schouwburgplein can be a pleasant rendezvous regardless of the weather. The four largest auditoria are raised above the square and form a spectacular urban roofscape while the three smaller ones form a plinth for the foyer. Because it rests on an existing underground car park, the cinema's structure is as lightweight as possible, with an outer shell made of lightweight corrugated plastic panels that glow at night.

The local government building (1994–97) in Terneuzen is an extension of the existing town hall designed by Bakema in 1972, a brutalist concrete structure with a tower overlooking the busy traffic on the River Schelde like a ship's bridge. At first sight it seems that van Velsen has simply placed a new office tower block at a respectable distance from the older building, but the two buildings are in fact linked by a subterranean structure, with offices grouped around sunken patios. This solution preserves a view of the church from the dyke and of the Schelde from De Kolk, and the two buildings now mark the corners of the new civic square, Stadshuisplein. The hefty mass of Bakema's town hall, with its expressive form and prosaic materials, seems to float oddly above the ground, catching the reflection of the changing skies in its façades.

Academy of Arts (Rijksakademie), Amsterdam
Ground-floor plan, longitudinal section

Academy of Arts (Rijksakademie), Amsterdam
Photography studio

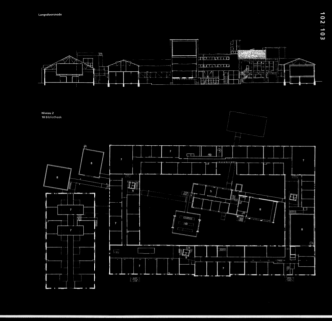

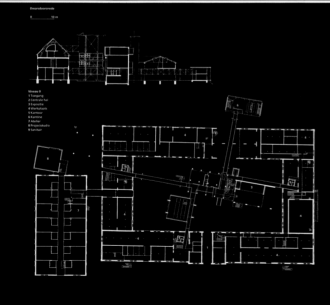

Academy of Arts (Rijksakademie), Amsterdam
Second-floor plan, cross section

Academy of Arts (Rijksakademie), Amsterdam
View of library building from a corridor in the existing building

Academy of Arts (Rijksakademie), Amsterdam
Offices in courtyard

Town Hall, Terneuzen
View towards the Schelde river

Town Hall, Terneuzen
View from the frozen Schelde river

Town Hall, Terneuzen
View of extension

Town Hall, Terneuzen
Ground-level plan

Town Hall, Terneuzen
Third-level plan of exension

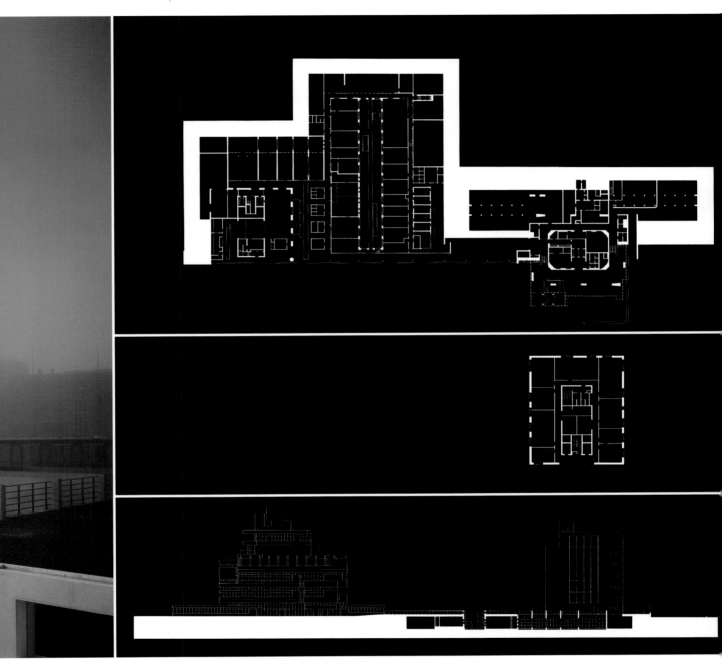

Town Hall, Terneuzen
Longitudinal and cross sections

Town Hall, Terneuzen
Patio in new extension

Borneo Sporenburg Urban Plan, Amsterdam
Model

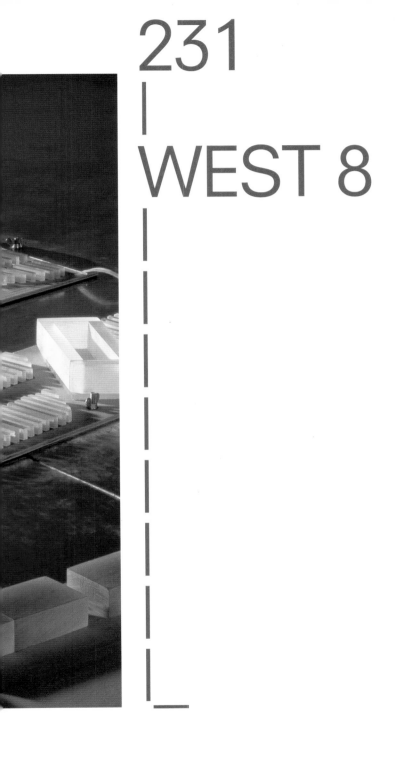

231
|
WEST 8

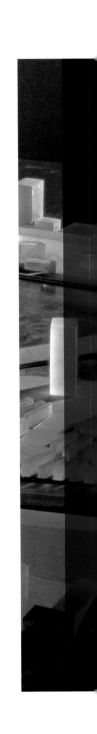

Schouwburgplein, Rotterdam
Aerial view during public event

It is largely to the credit of Adriaan Geuze and West 8 that landscape architecture has reappeared on the agenda of the Dutch architectural discourse. On the one hand, West 8 situates itself in the longstanding functionalist and pragmatic tradition of Dutch landscape architecture. On the other hand, the firm realizes that the trend towards individualization and the rising population density, mobility and welfare, implies a wholly new landscape use in the Netherlands. The distinction between town and country, in particular between town and nature, has become blurred. In West 8's view, the landscape should no longer be regarded as the counterform of the city, but as the entire configuration of town and country and the people who inhabit them. As Geuze puts it, 'The new city is an airy metropolis, with villages, urban centres, suburbs, industrial zones, docks, airports, forests, lakes, beaches, nature reserves and the monocultural acreages of high-tech agriculture.' West 8 accordingly concerns itself with this entire spectrum, from small gardens and patios within architectural projects to the design of public urban spaces, from such major planning projects as the landscaping of Schiphol Airport to town-planning schemes and the design of large-scale land reclamations (in the best Dutch tradition). As a whole, this approach is consistent with post-war planning practice in the Netherlands, in which landscape architects have been involved from the outset in the planning for the *tabula rasa* of the new polders.

In West 8's view, the landscape of parks and natural areas has a primarily ecological significance as suggested in the traditional, romantic conception of landscape architecture rather than merely being a recompense for the stress-laden city dweller. The urban inhabitant is not 'the pitiful victim of the city who needs looking after and protecting in a gentle, green environment', as Geuze states, but a self-assured individual who seeks out the places he wishes to go to for his chosen activities, even when those places are far away. Furthermore, the range of people's activities during their free time has expanded vastly over the last twenty years.

In the urban scheme for Borneo and Sporenburg (1994–present), two districts in the eastern part of Amsterdam's harbour, West 8 offers an answer to the paradox that has become a common issue in urban design projects in the Netherlands. How can one satisfy the requirement for a housing density of 100 units per hectare, while making as many dwellings as possible low-rise homes with individual gardens? West 8 sought to solve the problem by developing new dwelling types, with patios and roof gardens, each conceived as an intimate, private base for exploration of a wider area. They allocated a large portion of the plan area, which would conventionally be assigned to public space, to be included within the dwellings, with the resulting denser urban texture being compensated for by the wide expanses of water around the peninsulas. The water is visible not only from the quays but from the roof gardens and from several high pedestrian footbridges, while the sea of houses is treated as

Schouwburgplein, Rotterdam
Night view with illuminated fountains

Schouwburgplein, Rotterdam
Fountains and the bench in the evening sun

a landscape in which three large residential blocks are aligned towards crucial points in the surrounding landscape. The blocks give the inhabitants a panoramic view, but they also serve to anchor Borneo and Sporenburg to the surrounding landscape. Because West 8 wanted to provide a greater variety of dwellings than the swathes of identical houses that the Dutch building system tends to produce, commissions to individual architects were spread in smaller units over the whole plan area.

Schouwburgplein (1991–96) in Rotterdam, was designed as a raised platform on which Geuze's 'active citizen' can optimally manifest himself. The square is flanked by three large theatres: the Schouwburg, the De Doelen concert hall and a new multiplex cinema designed by Koen van Velsen (pages 216–19). The platform is a lightweight metal structure supported on the roof of an existing underground car park and is bathed in green and blue light from below. Four spotlight units are mounted on hydraulic masts, which members of the public can activate from a coin-operated control. The lights can be used to illuminate an informal night-time football match, for example, or to add zest to a demonstration of roller skating or skateboarding. In addition, the platform has a large number of electrical connections and mechanical anchoring points to accommodate street markets, fairgrounds, circuses or an open-air cinema. A long bench alongside the square and a terrace with open-air cafés provide seating places for people to watch what is happening on the platform. West 8 chose not to emphasize the boundaries of the platform in any way (apart from the height difference relative to the surrounding streets), since it would eventually be visually contained by the skyline rapidly rising around it.

While Schouwburgplein is an unorthodox solution to an ostensibly classic location, the urban square, Carrascoplein (1992–97), near Sloterdijk Station in Amsterdam, is nothing like a city square. It is what Marc Augé terms a non-place, a no-man's land among and underneath a tangle of main roads, tramways and railways in the urban periphery. The original brief was to design a park there, but it would have been in the shade for most of the day and the need for car parks would have taken up much of the surface area. West 8 thus proposed a mixture of 'creative parking' and low-maintenance greenery, with black asphalt and lawns laid out in an expressive pattern reminiscent of Burle Marx. Planted in the lawns are cast-iron tree stumps with lamps that illuminate the undersides of the concrete viaducts, which dramatizes the space. A pier of one of the viaducts has been transformed into a concrete tree entwined in concrete lianas (woody, climbing plants).

The garden of the Interpolis insurance company building (1995–97) in Tilburg, on the other hand, is almost a classic piece of park design. The garden occupies an inner-city site bordered on one side by an office building by Abe Bonnema and giving access on the other side to a popular new music auditorium and car park by Benthem and Crouwel. The park provides an alternative route for pedestrians walking from the railway station to the city centre.

Schouwburgplein, Rotterdam
View showing Koen van Velsen's Megacinema (left)

A row of large flagstones provides a transition from the garden to Bonnema's building, and a series of monumental pools leads the way from the building to the city centre. The edges of the pools also function as benches, where the Interpolis employees can enjoy their lunch. They can even do their work there: instead of fixed desk locations office staff are provided with portable workstations (a kind of suitcase on castors) containing a notebook computer and mobile telephone.

Schouwburgplein, Rotterdam
Use of the square by day: a stage for the people of Rotterdam

Interpolis Gardens, Tilburg
Plan

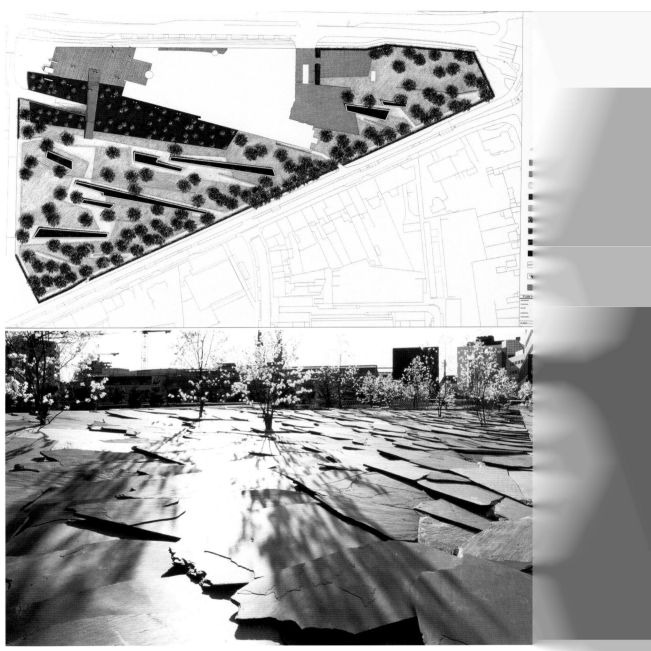

Interpolis Gardens, Tilburg
Detail of stone garden

Carrascoplein, Amsterdam
Night view

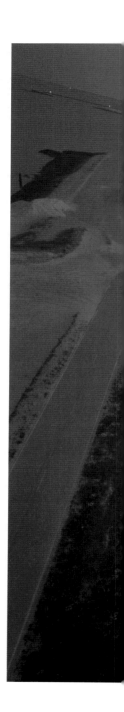

Oosterscheldedam Flood Barrier, Zeeland
View of bird reservation

AMNESTY FOR THE REAL WORLD

INDIVIDUALIZATION

The practice of communal architecture and planning in the Netherlands stands in growing contrast to the individualization that is becoming increasingly prevalent in our ever more globalized society. Sociologists, such as Ulrich Beck and Anthony Giddens, see individualization as a key aspect of the 'second modernity' and as an inevitable and necessary stage on the way to new forms of society. In industrial society, there were direct relationships between social class, the family, sexual role patterns, marriage, the division of labour between men and women and architectural typologies. Today more and more people have the opportunity (or are forced) to replace the standard life plan by a 'do-it-yourself biography', as Ronald Hitzler calls it, or in Giddens's terms, 'a reflexive biography'. According to Ulrich Beck, individualization means: 'First, the disembedding and, second, the re-embedding of industrial society and replacing old ways of life by new ones, in which the individuals must cobble together, produce and stage their biographies themselves.'[1] Beck sees the emergence of individualization as a 1970s trend, a consequence of increasing prosperity and higher levels of education in the Western welfare states, of which the Netherlands was a prime example in many respects. These factors gave people greater individual political awareness and confidence, and as a result they demanded a more active voice in society. This new popular involvement was initially aimed at the protection and expansion of the individual, small-scale domain.

Beck theorizes that if society continues to grow ever more congested, people will automatically realize the need for more sweeping measures to achieve new forms of collectivity – but this will only be possible because of the individual's awareness of this need. Beck cites the example of a billboard alongside a usually traffic-jammed motorway near Munich that bears the message, 'You aren't in a jam, you are the jam'. The sign aims to instill exactly the kind of awareness Beck has in mind.[2]

Remarkably, in the Netherlands an entirely contrary development appears to be taking place. While the architecture and planning of the early 1990s featured successive attempts to establish compact forms of collectivity within which individuality would be nurtured in an introverted fashion, the transition to the new millennium has been marked by a development approach in which entire suburbs are realized in a single design gesture. As a result of the desire to take individualization seriously, there is also an increasing resistance to an architecture that focuses on design in the first instance.

HABITATION GONE WILD:
'HET WILDE WONEN'

Adriaan Geuze and West 8 set the cat among the pigeons when they launched their 'Wilderness' scheme as part of AIR 1993 ('AIR Alexander, New Urban Frontiers'). Rather than suggesting another suburban development cluster they advocated scattering individual houses across the green heart of the Randstad, with each house on an extremely large plot of land so that at least the ecological function of the Randstad's foliage would be preserved.[3] MVRDV followed suit with their 'Light Urbanism' plan, which not only aspired to a similar ultralow density development for the Midden-IJsselmonde district near Rotterdam but proposed the idea of a literally lighter, cheaper and more ephemeral architecture and infrastructure so that large individual building plots could be retained.[4] The market was particularly pleased that the subject of individual housing was now open to discussion. After all, the demand had existed for a long time but it had rarely been satisfied.

In 1997 the national newspaper NRC Handelsblad published an interview with the then chairman of the Federation of Dutch Architects (BNA), Carel Weeber. He argued strongly for abandoning the preconceived image in urban design and instead endorsed dividing the developable land area into smaller plots on which people could build individual houses relatively inexpensively. The houses need not be designed by architects, but could

1. Ulrich Beck, 'The Reinvention of Politics', in: Ulrich Beck, Anthony Giddens, Scott Lash, Reflexive Modernization, Politics, Tradition and Aesthetics in the Modern Social Order (Cambridge/Oxford, 1994).
2. Idem.

3. Adriaan Geuze/West 8, 'Wildernis', in Anne Mie Devolder (ed.), Alexanderpolder, waar de stad verder gaat (Bussum, 1993)
4. MVRDV, 'Lichte Stedebouw', in Cees Boekraad and Wim van Es (eds), Rotterdam 2045, Visies op de toekomst van stad, haven en regio (Rotterdam, 1995)

be constructed by the residents themselves from off-the-shelf mass-produced modules.[5] Weeber called this style of development '*Het Wilde Wonen*', or 'Wild Housing'. Prior to the publication of Weeber's interview, architects, urbanists and politicians reacted strongly against ideas of this kind, but luxury detached house developments had already proliferated, especially on the outskirts of provincial towns, a phenomenon known disparagingly as 'white fungus' on account of the predominant colour of the masonry.

Weeber's contention, which was in line with his earlier calls for the abolition of *Welstandstoezicht* (the official control of the appearance of buildings), had a tremendous impact. The criticism from professional circles was exhaustive and impassioned, not only because of the risk of endless sprawl and uncontrolled expansion of towns but because it was unprecedented for a chairman of the BNA to attack the profession in such a way. In effect he was pronouncing the obsolescence of architecture and planning. But there was also plenty of support, particularly in political circles. The Dutch Labour Party parliamentarian and former director of the Netherlands Architecture Institute, Adri Duivesteijn, proposed taking a similar approach to provide affordable homes to lower-income families as a way of breaking the stranglehold of the housing corporations, property developers and construction companies.[6]

The sense of timing with which Weeber premiered his *Wilde Wonen* idea was perfect: the consequences of the trend towards deregulation that the government had been following since the late 1980s were becoming more and more apparent, the country's economic position had greatly improved, the financial deficit was strongly reduced, unemployment was declining, individual prosperity was rising and the Dutch 'polder model' economy was widely admired internationally. The result was a kind of euphoria, with many people arguing that deregulation was not going far enough, and that it wasn't just the laws and regulations that were impeding major economic expansion

and cramping individual freedom but the endless rounds of consultation.

FREE ZONES
Thus, in 1997, when Carel Weeber made his public case for the deregulation of house-building, several other architects and artists began advancing far-reaching deregulation proposals. That same year, OMA published a booklet called *MAA$VLAKTE* (referring to the Maasvlakte Docks district of Rotterdam), the outcome of a study commissioned by the economic research forum *NYFER* on the expansion of the Rotterdam harbour. They proposed detaching the harbour economically and legally from the city to establish a 'free zone' on the model of Singapore and the special economic zones of China, which would enable the harbour to change and expand more quickly and enhance its competitiveness within Europe. Decoupling the harbour from the rest of the city would also, in OMA's view, augment the identity of the city. One of the recommendations of the study was not to rehabilitate the city's pre-war housing stock, which was ripe for renovation, but to demolish it, which would make way for new experiments and so embrace Carel Weeber's proposals.[7]

In 1997, too, Adriaan Geuze and West 8 laid out a provocative exhibition in the Groninger Museum (in the section designed by Coop Himmelb(l)au), which was not only an ode to postwar reconstruction but a proposal to create three gigantic 'free zones' in the Netherlands: one centred around the harbour of Rotterdam, another around Amsterdam, and a third occupying the southernmost tip of the Netherlands, near Maastricht. These zones, whose existence would help the Netherlands keep up with the United States and the tiger economies of Asia, would be managed by a new Ministry of Innovation and Acceleration, while the rest of the country would be under the aegis of the Ministry of Consolidation and Self-Satisfaction, where time could stand still while the inhabitants benefited from the accelerating regions of the Netherlands.[8]

To cap it all, the following year Atelier van Lieshout launched a non-theoretical proposal to establish a self-

5. Bernard Hulsman, 'Het wilde wonen, Carel Weeber wil af van het rijtjeshuis', *NRC Handelsblad, Cultureel Supplement* 4–4–1997, p. 1.
6. Wouter Vanstiphout, 'Naar Wilde Plannen', in Carel Weeber, *Het Wilde Wonen* (Rotterdam, 1998)

7. Office for Metropolitan Architecture/NYFER Forum for Economic Research, *MAA$VLAKTE* (The Hague, 1997).
8. Adriaan Geuze and West 8, *90.000 pakjes margarine, 100 meter vooruit, West 8 over landschap in acceleratie* (exh. cat.) (Groningen, 1997).

governing community under the leadership of van Lieshout himself. AVL-Ville, as it was to be called, would be sited on the former chemical-waste dump under the landing approach to Rotterdam's Zestienhoven Airport. The drawings show AVL-Ville as a cross between a Shaker community and a Hell's Angels clubhouse, replete with weapons and custom trucks. Moreover, the community would house the workshops for fabricating weapons, liquor and medicines that the Atelier has since constructed. This scheme occupies a clear place within van Lieshout's oeuvre and could be regarded as a successor to the caravans he built in the studio, but the idea also extends to collective residences with sufficient space for van Lieshout's 'Multi-Woman Beds'. A small clinic (complete with operating theatre), a chicken coop, an electricity generator, livestock sheds and several other aspects have already been built. When Atelier van Lieshout presented the scheme under the title of 'The Good, The Bad and The Ugly' in the small French town of Rabastens in 1998, the mayor ordered the exhibition to be closed down after only three days,[9] an act that was obviously contrary to the freedom of speech and of art. Yet it is curious that in the same period, and with little ado, the municipality of Rotterdam offered a site for realizing AVL-Ville, starting in 2002.

It remains to be seen what would happen if van Lieshout really did start distilling alcohol, manufacturing medicines, performing medical treatments or defending these activities with self-made armaments. Things would no doubt sort themselves out, as the criminologist Peter Hoefnagels wrote in the catalogue of 'The Good, The Bad and The Ugly'.[10] But although one of the main themes of Atelier van Lieshout's work is its deadly serious research into the point at which the freedom of the individual is curtailed, nobody in the Netherlands takes that research at face value or knows quite what to make of it. The country's reputed tradition of tolerance has had an official sanction in which the authorities keep a watchful eye on certain formally illegal activities, such as prostitution and soft drugs, without actively trying to eliminate them. These areas of tolerance have always been specific exceptions to the rule. Now it looks as though the exceptions are about to become the rule.

NEW ARCHITECTURE PRACTICES

It is against this background of a market shaped by progressive deregulation and individualization that a range of new architecture practices are emerging. These aspects were clearly of great importance to the generation of architects and theorists who rose so emphatically to prominence in the 1990s, but their approaches were still marked by a remembrance of the struggle of the period before that; their efforts were directed at devising ingenious strategies to preserve as much design quality as possible within the new system. Consisting mainly of collectives or collaborating groups of architects, planners, architectural historians, industrial designers and artists, this new generation of architecture practices, in contrast, has opted for freedom and adventure.

Rem Koolhaas and to a lesser extent Carel Weeber and Adriaan Geuze form the main points of reference for these new practices. I write Rem Koolhaas and not OMA, for in most cases it is not a matter of a formal reference to OMA's designs or completed projects but mainly of Koolhaas's theory and research. His principal influence is his rejection of architecture that is driven chiefly by the will to create architectonic form. Geuze, who takes the credit for being the first to point out how individualization was beginning to manifest itself, spoke as long ago as 1993 of the 'sensation of the unprogrammed' in an influential essay titled 'Accelerating Darwin'. In his analysis of the sandy wasteland around the Maasvlakte, he notes that it accommodates a variety of industrial complexes, whose presence would not be tolerated elsewhere owing to their potential environmental nuisance, and yet this unlikely area is crowded with tourists at weekends and public holidays. It is a popular place for motocross, autocross, hang-gliding, diving practice and picnicking. Geuze emphasizes

9. Atelier van Lieshout, *The Good, The Bad and The Ugly* (Rotterdam, 1998).
10. Ibid.

Max.1
General model of Leidsche Rijn

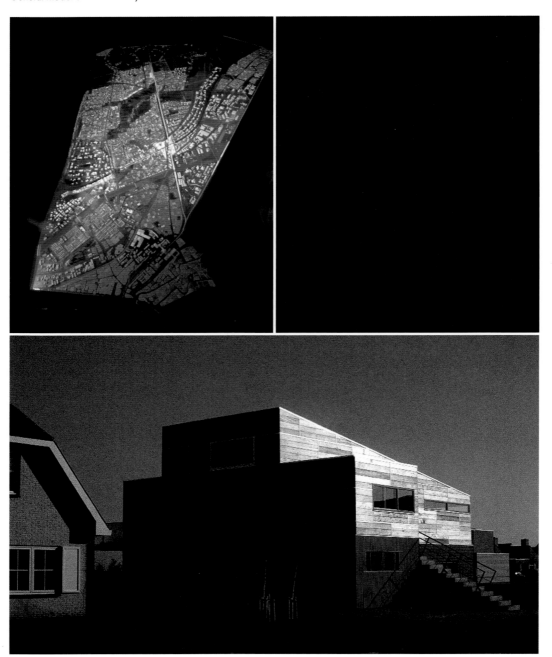

Max.1
The Ugliest House in the Netherlands, Leeuwarden (1994)

NL.Architects
WOS 8, Leidsche Rijn (1998)

NL.Architects
Climbers on the practice wall of WOS 8

that the design of new public space is not a matter of formal design, of 'the beauty of proportions, materials and colours', but of 'the sensation of a spontaneous culture, which the city-dweller creates'.[11]

In a situation that is increasingly shaped by the market and by individualization, Koolhaas's and Geuze's rejection of formal design has turned out to be far-sighted. All imaginable styles, each stranger than the last, thrive in parallel. This is due in part to the choices made by the architects, but also because clients are becoming more certain of what they want and are prepared to demand it. Given the speed at which new neighbourhoods are being constructed in the Netherlands, neither tradition nor fashion is capable of exerting a regulating effect. A broader cohesion can not be achieved in ensembles except by artificial, contrived means. One problem with today's architecture is that alongside a stunning building that makes it to the pages of the architecture magazines, someone can come and erect a Heidi-style chalet. What is more, modern architecture stands out like a sore thumb amid the 'farmette' and eccentric shams. In this situation, there is a danger that architecture, which has long been the defender of more general, higher cultural values, will lose its significance. That is why Koolhaas, Geuze and their new crop of followers are seeking new strategies for planning and urban management.

MAX.1

The most important representative of this new group is perhaps Max.1, consisting of Rients Dijkstra and Rianne Makkink. The practice made its first showing in 1994 with a simple house in Leeuwarden (which I published at the time as 'The Ugliest House in the Netherlands'),[12] a modern villa residence in a typical new neighbourhood consisting otherwise solely of tasteless farmettes. The architects aimed to give the house a striking profile against the surrounding landscape by inverting the standard typology: the spacious living room is upstairs and the bedrooms downstairs. The house thus bears no

resemblance whatsoever to its neighbours, except that many of the exterior materials were 'sampled' from the surrounding area. Its flagrant mismatch with other houses in the locality make it clear that it was meant as a deliberate provocation.

In the period that Dijkstra and Makkink designed the house, the former was still employed at OMA, where he was responsible for the firm's most invisible project, the tram tunnel in The Hague. Max.1 became a definitive reality when Dijkstra and Makkink won a commission to design the master plan for a development of no less than 30,000 homes for one of the largest VINEX locations, Leidsche Rijn near Utrecht. Because prior research was clearly a vital activity for a development on this gigantic scale, one of the first steps Dijkstra and Makkink took was to bring in Crimson (see below), a collective of architectural historians, to provide support on the preliminary design. The historians were not restricted to research, however, for they were also actively involved in devising the urban plan. The size of the development and the knowledge that at least 70 per cent of the dwellings would be unsubsidized and hence market-dependent meant that it would be impossible to take an idealized approach. The Leidsche Rijn site overlaps several municipalities, each of which wished to retain some independent say in the development, so the planners placed a large park in the middle of the site. Besides functioning as a central urban green area, the park, designed by West 8, separates the individual municipal territories. On the Utrecht side, the development connects as directly as possible to the existing city centre by building over part of the A2 highway – a design decision that is unarguably the most expensive and difficult to realize. The entire district is unusual in that the traffic infrastructure is not separated from the residential neighbourhoods but forms an integral part of the environment. Max.1 aim, in their own words, to scatter the houses over the area like a powder, while trying to create diversity in the development by applying relatively simple

11. Adriaan Geuze, 'Accelerating Darwin', in Gerrit Smienk (ed.), *Nederlandse Landschapsarchitectuur, tussen traditie en experiment* (Amsterdam, 1993).

12. Bart Lootsma, 'Het lelijkste huis van Nederland, Villa Max1. In Leeuwarden van Rianne Makkink en Rients Dijkstra', *de Architect*, no. 3, 1994

rules for varying density, levels of aesthetic control, maximum building heights and design styles. Leidsche Rijn is currently under construction.

NL.ARCHITECTS

Consisting of Pieter Bannenberg, Walter van Dijk, Kamiel Klaasse and Mark Linneman, the Amsterdam-based collective NL.Architects first drew attention to themselves with a number of provocative designs for the city of Amsterdam, in which they opted decisively for commercial forces as the mainspring of their ideas. Their 'Parkhouse.Carstadt' proposal, for example, involved creating a huge car-park landscape in the historic city centre on the Museumplein public square, designed so that the parked vehicles would form the letters 'MAZDA' when seen from above. Parking could be free here since the hypothetical sponsor would meet the cost. Other ideas included changing parts of the city's canals into swimming pools and introducing travelling supermarkets on trains.

The first built design by NL.Architects was the WOS 8 heat-exchanger station of 1998, part of the district heating system in Leidsche Rijn – at first sight WOS 8 is a self-enclosed, monolithic black block with rounded corners. On further examination, however, the building reveals several pleasing details: there are nesting boxes for birds under the roof edges and a roosting area for bats; the north façade supports a basketball hoop whose transparent backing board provides the building's only window; the east elevation has a pattern of roadside reflectors that form the building's name when illuminated by vehicle headlights; the west elevation is studded with grips to make it a practice wall for rock climbers; the south side has a large opening through which rainwater gushes in a spectacular way, a basketball landing on the roof will also roll out through this aperture. Added to the function of the building as a distribution point for heat, these features make it into a monument to the communal spirit of the neighbourhood, while responding subtly to the demands of individualization.

ONE ARCHITECTURE

The most unpredictable and eccentric new group to make its presence felt in recent years is One Architecture, consisting of Matthijs Bouw and Joost Meuwissen, also based in Amsterdam. As the editor of the Dutch magazine *Plan* in the 1970s, the older partner, Meuwissen, was an established critic and theorist. He introduced countless foreign architects and theorists to the Dutch architectural scene and helped Dutch architecture catch up internationally in that period. In the 1980s he founded a periodical of his own, the brilliant but idiosyncratic magazine *Wiederhall* (entirely in the English language), of which nineteen issues appeared. He is a professor and dean of the faculty of urban planning at the University of Technology of Graz, Austria.

Meuwissen formed an association with the much younger Bouw in 1994. Bouw had attracted attention in 1992, when he was twenty-five, by helping design an anarchist nursery in Soest, in collaboration with Ton Venhoeven and others. As One Architecture, they caused a stir with study designs for Leidsche Rijn, which contained such provocative ideas as building tennis courts on top of houses, and a series of conceptual projects that deliberately tested the limits of deception and parody. They subsequently won a competition for a housing development near Salzburg in Austria, which is currently under construction.

The members of One Architecture recognize their indebtedness to the thinking of Rem Koolhaas, but they also draw inspiration from such architects as Giorgio Grassi and Friedrich Schinkel and from such artists as Berend Strik, with whom they collaborate regularly. The influence of the artist Jeff Koons is even more significant. His early 'appropriation art', in which he deployed common consumer articles (vacuum cleaners, basketballs) to set up complex references to art history, thereby elevating them to the realm of high culture, does suggest a striking analogy with the way Koolhaas took banal urban phenomena and typologies seriously and incorporated them into a new mythology,

One Architecture
Private house, near Eindhoven (1999)

Bas Princen

as in his book *Delirious New York*.[13] Koons later did the same with objects drawn from the broad domain of kitsch and 'bad taste', such as porcelain piglets, cherubs, folk wood carvings, pornography, Michael Jackson and comic-strip heroes, which he blew up to monumental proportions and had executed in expensive materials. Koons's aim was to make 'high' art accessible and attractive to the public while showing that it was nonetheless possible to play an intellectual game with it.

In their design for an extension to a private house near Eindhoven, One Architecture followed a strategy similar to that of Koons. Fifteen years previously the client had commissioned a house in a French country style, which was surrounded by a huge plot of land. The house no longer met the lifestyle needs of the client and his family. When asked to carry out alterations to the house, One Architecture did not offer a sketch design, rather they presented the client with a brochure of sample house designs in styles ranging from Palladio to Ben van Berkel and asked him to select one. The favoured design proved to be Mies van der Rohe's Farnsworth House. Accordingly, One Architecture's eventual design was a Miesian pavilion that intersects with the existing house, with materials and engineering adapted to contemporary standards. The classic stainless-steel cornice contains a five-metre retractable canopy, motors to operate the sliding glass walls and curtains, heating, illumination and electrostatic insect traps. The brilliant curtain that can be drawn over the whole front of the house, was designed by Berend Strik.

CRIMSON

The members of Crimson, Michelle Provoost, Wouter Vanstiphout, Ewout Dorman, Cassandra Wilkins and Ernst van der Hoeven, studied architectural history under Ed Taverne at Groningen University. As Crimson, they do what architectural historians normally do: historical research, tasks related to the listing and preservation of historic buildings, writing articles, compiling books and curating exhibitions. One example of their recent output

(in collaboration with the American theorist Michael Speaks and the designer Gerard Hadders) is a book provocatively titled *Mart Stam's Trousers: Stories from Behind the Scenes of Dutch Moral Modernism*, which follows Rem Koolhaas in poking fun at the small-minded Calvinistic moralism and hypocrisy of Dutch modern architecture.[14] But it is not all research and theory for Crimson, they have explicit contact with the building process itself. This may not seem all that unusual in as far as it relates to architectural criticism or the aesthetic input to the planning process as participants in the *Welstandscommissies* (Architectural Review Committees). The latter capacity has become fairly standard in the Netherlands since most committees include a historic buildings expert or historian, but the members of Crimson are not shy of taking part in the design process itself, or even making their own designs. For example, they make programme proposals for the alteration or renovation of historic buildings and recent monuments.

They see their work as a form of resistance against what they call the 'red haze' that long fogged the vision of Dutch social-democratic local governments in their efforts to redesign and embellish entire cities. This, in Crimson's view, is a politically biased and heavy-handed approach to planning that suppresses the spontaneous energy and creativity of the inhabitants. Crimson prefers to look to peripheral areas and margins to which planning has not yet penetrated and where spontaneous and perhaps even illegal developments are taking place. They hope to stimulate these forces with minimal means, such as simple changes in the regulations, which they call 'Orgware'.

The Org-Wars project is a mixture of research and design commissioned by the Rotterdam Department of Housing and Town Planning, for which Crimson supplied a variety of strategies for the city's future development. The project is based on the observation that town planning has almost reached the limits of its capacities as a design discipline and has been replaced by an urbanism in which each project has to be negotiated to an ad hoc

13. Rem Koolhaas, *Delirious New York* (London/ New York, 1978).

14. Crimson, with Michael Speaks and Gerard Hadders, *Mart Stam's Trousers: Stories from Behind the Scenes of Dutch Moral Modernism* (Rotterdam, 1999).

consensus involving many different parties. Crimson's statement captures their thinking: 'The Rotterdam project means stumbling in on the treasures of the urbanism of negotiation; it is an investigation into how ideas can be distilled from the existing city and how they can be formatted to have maximum influence. In the end it is about building the ideal city, about trusting contemporary reality to supply us with its ingredients, instead of the discipline of design or the power of state.'[15]

AMNESTY FOR THE REAL WORLD

If Crimson closely approaches an 'amnesty for the real world', that is, a standpoint of accepting the existing character of the built environment and the social and economic conditions that have given rise to it, the same is perhaps even more true for a number of designers who concern themselves explicitly with the problems of planning and urban design. Buro Schie, for example, established in 1991 by Lucas Verwey and Ton Matton, is concerned with a broad variety of projects, collaborating by preference with a team of representatives from other disciplines. Projects may take the form of future scenarios or of strategies for art commissioning in connection with new housing developments, but they are also sometimes detailed architectural or urban design proposals. The most appealing of these, however, are the projects in which the way they represent a situation changes the perception of it so drastically that the result could be regarded as a design. For instance, Buro Schie's New Map of the Netherlands, commissioned by the BNS (Federation of Dutch Town Planners), shows all the extant building plans in the Netherlands. The most remarkable example of Buro Schie's work, however, is the Randstad Straten Plattegrond (Randstad Street Plan). Simply by representing the entire conglomerate of cities that form the Randstad in a unified street plan with daytime and night-time maps of the main public transport services, they make it clear at a glance that the Randstad has indeed long been a single city which is used by its inhabitants like those in London or Paris.
Another important contribution to

the thinking about urban planning are the photographs made by Bas Princen, who, like Verwey, studied at the Design Academy in Eindhoven before completing his training at the Berlage Institute in Amsterdam. There is nothing special about the scenes he depicts, at least at first sight. They are typical Dutch landscapes, generally flat, artificial and often still lacking a clear function – ostensibly forgotten landscapes in the periphery of the city or in the periphery of nature. Oddly enough, however, it is precisely because of this uncertainty that these landscapes have attracted a wide group of people who use them for activities for which there is no room or which are not tolerated elsewhere. These activities are mainly in the sphere of leisure: autocross and motocross, all kinds of racing, picnicking and simply meandering. The minor physical changes the participants make in the landscape will have as good as disappeared after the first shower of rain, activities like those to which Adriaan Geuze drew attention on the Maasvlakte. Perhaps it is a result of the contrast with the surrounding emptiness, but the conditions that Princen photographs radiate an incredible vitality. Princen does not consider his photographs as mere documentation bu as design projects: in an exhibition in Breda, the photographs became gigantic blow-ups presented in similar situations to those in which the shots were taken. More than anything, the billboards recall the large signs building contractors place in green fields when they start work on a project – with the difference that it is not an artist's impression of a future building but a photograph of a real situation somewhere.

The amnesty for the real built environment for which the very latest generation of Dutch architects and urbanists stands is certainly not an uncritical one. To some extent their work suggests a potentially liberating critique of customary forms of architecture and urbanism. But it is quite a different critique from that which, for example, the Situationists had in mind when they tried to escape the power of urbanism. They may aim for the victory

15. Crimson, 'Org-Wars, Post-urban Strategies by the Dutch Group Crimson', *Daidalos,* no. 72, 1999.

of everyday life, but that does not make it a victory over the capitalist system, which emerges more strongly than ever. Guy Debord, the leader of the Situationists, argued in 'The Society of the Spectacle' that capitalism, if it were to become global, would lead to a trivialization and a homogenization of space, but so far only the former appears to be the case.[16] The system has adapted faster than Debord and his followers could have imagined to the individualization of society, and may even have helped bring this about (contrary to what he predicted), thereby absorbing the ideas of its critics, as has so often happened in the past. The major task facing Dutch architecture in the years ahead will be to give a concrete shape to the new forms of collectivity – to reconcile the Heidi chalet with the van Berkel villa. Unlike in the work of the previous generation, there is not much prospect of that happening yet.

16. Guy Debord, *The Society of the Spectacle* (New York, 1994).

WIEL ARETS

Born in Heerlen in 1955, Arets graduated from the Eindhoven University of Technology in 1983 and started his own firm in Heerlen almost immediately afterwards. The practice is currently based in Maastricht. Arets's most important projects include the Academy of Arts and Architecture in Maastricht (1989–93), the AZL Pensionfund building in Heerlen (1990–95), police stations in Vaals (1993–95), Cuijck (1994–97), Boxtel (1994–97) and Heerlen (1994–97) and the Lensvelt offices and factory in Breda (1997–99). Projects under construction or in preparation include apartment buildings in Rotterdam (1992–2000), the university library in Utrecht (1997–2002), a cathedral in Ghana (1998–2002) and a multifunctional football stadium in Groningen (1998–2002). Dean of the Berlage Institute in Amsterdam since 1995, Arets has also lectured at the Architectural Association in London, Columbia University in New York, the Hochschule für Angewandte Kunst in Vienna and the Royal Danish Academy of Fine Arts in Copenhagen, as well as holding the Cátedra Mies van der Rohe at Barcelona University. His buildings have been the subject of numerous magazine articles and several monographs, including *Wiel Arets, Architect* by Manfred Bock (Rotterdam, 1998) and an issue of *El Croquis* (no. 85, 1997).

UN STUDIO (VAN BERKEL & BOS)

Ben van Berkel (born in Utrecht, 1957) graduated from the Architectural Association in London in 1987; Caroline Bos (born in Rotterdam, 1959) graduated in art history from Birkbeck College, London. They established Van Berkel & Bos Architectuurbureau in Amsterdam and transformed the practice into the network organization UN Studio in 1998. Together van Berkel and Bos teach at the Berlage Institute, Amsterdam, and since 2000 have jointly held a visiting professorship at Princeton University; van Berkel has also lectured at Columbia University, New York, and the Architectural Association in London. Their most important projects are the REMU 50/10kV distribution substation in Amersfoort (1989–93), the office/industrial building for Karbouw in Amersfoort (1990–92), the Erasmus Bridge in Rotterdam (1990–96), Villa Wilbrink in Amersfoort (1992–94), the conversion and extension of Rijksmuseum Twente in Enschede (1996), the Möbius House in Naarden (1993–98) and Museum Het Valkhof in Nijmegen (1995–99). Projects under construction or in preparation include the station zone in

Arnhem (1998–), the NMR Facilities Laboratory of the University of Utrecht (1996–2000) and the faculty of music building in Graz, Austria (1998–2002). Numerous publications about the work of Van Berkel & Bos/UN Studio have appeared, including a special issue of *El Croquis* (no. 72). Van Berkel and Bos have themselves published many theoretical and critical articles and several books, including *Delinquent Visionaries* (Rotterdam, 1993), *Mobile Forces* (Berlin, 1994) and *Move* (Amsterdam, 1999).

ERICK VAN EGERAAT

Born in Amsterdam in 1956, van Egeraat graduated from the architecture department of Delft University of Technology in 1984. He was a partner in Mecanoo Architecten in Delft from 1983 to 1995, then moved to Rotterdam to found EEA (Erick van Egeraat Associated Architects). The most important projects built by the latter practice include the ING/Nationale Nederlanden building in Budapest (1992–97), the Huygens Laboratory of the Leiden University astronomy and physics department (1993–97), the Crawford Municipal Art Gallery in Cork, Ireland (1996–2000), the Ichtus Hogeschool in Rotterdam (1996–2000) and the Royal Shakespeare Theatre in Stratford-upon-Avon (1998–2004). In 1997 van Egeraat published the book *Six Ideas about Architecture (Sechs Anmerkungen zur Architektur)*, with text by Deyan Sudjic (Basle, Boston, Berlin, 1997).

ATELIER VAN LIESHOUT

Joep van Lieshout (born in Ravenstein, 1963) graduated from Rotterdam's Hogeschool voor de Kunsten in 1985. He then spent two years at Ateliers '63 in Haarlem. Since then his artistic practice has developed into Atelier van Lieshout, located in Rotterdam with a staff ranging from ten o twenty people. Atelier van Lieshout has been represented in countless solo and group exhibitions. His work is included in the collections of the Boijmans van Beuningen Museum in Rotterdam, the Stedelijk Museum in Amsterdam, the Kröller Müller Museum in Otterlo, the Museum für Gegenwartskunst in Zurich, the Museum of Modern Art in New York, the Van Abbemuseum in Eindhoven and the Walker Art Center in Minneapolis. His furnishings and architectural interventions appear in the Congrexpo in Lille (by OMA), the Museum of Modern Art in New York, Centraal Museum in Utrecht, the Walker Art Center in Minneapolis and on Pier G at Schiphol Airport, Amsterdam, among other places. The principal publications by Atelier van

Lieshout are *Atelier van Lieshout: A Manual* (Cologne, Rotterdam, Ostfildern, 1997) and *The Good, The Bad and The Ugly* (Rotterdam, 1998).

MECANOO

Since the firm was founded in 1984 in Delft the studio has had several line-ups. Of the original partners, Erick van Egeraat left the firm in 1995 and Chris de Weijer in 1998. Mecanoo currently still includes two founder members, Henk Döll (born Haarlem, 1956) and Francine Houben (born Sittard, 1956), who both graduated at the Delft University of Technology in 1984. Döll has been a visiting lecturer at the Berlage Institute in Amsterdam and the University of Technology in Vienna; Houben has had similar functions at Philadelphia University, the University of Calgary and the Berlage Institute. The firm's main completed projects include the student housing complex at Kruisplein, Rotterdam (1985), house and neighbourhood centre at De Hillekop in Rotterdam (1989), Restaurant De Boompjes in Rotterdam (1990), the Botanical Laboratory and the Library of the University of Wageningen (1992), the Prinsenland housing development in Rotterdam (1993), the public library in Almelo (1994), the Faculty of Economics and Management building of Hogeschool in Utrecht (1995) and the library of Delft University of Technology (1997). A monograph, *Mecanoo* (Rotterdam, 1995), was written by Kees Somer.

MVRDV

An acronym for 'Maas, van Rijs & de Vries', MVRDV's partners are Winy Maas (born Schijndel, 1959), Jacob van Rijs (born Amsterdam, 1964) and Nathalie de Vries (born Appingedam, 1965) and is based in Rotterdam. All three graduated from the Delft University of Technology in 1990; Winy Maas also studied landscape architecture at the RHSTL in Boskoop from 1978 to 1983. They have lectured at various universities and institutes in the Netherlands, including the Berlage Institute in Amsterdam, and abroad. Primary completed buildings are the three entry lodges of the Hoge Veluwe National Park (1996), Villa KBWW in Utrecht (1997, with Bjarne Mastenbroek), the WoZoCo development in Amsterdam (1997), the Radio Volks Universiteit headquarters and Villa VPRO, both in Hilversum (1997), the shared entrance building of Net 3 in Hilversum (2000) and the Dutch Pavilion at EXPO 2000 in Hanover. MVRDV's main publications are *Statics* (Rotterdam 1992), *FARMAX*

(Rotterdam, 1998), *MVRDV at VPRO* (Barcelona, 1999) and *Metacity/Datatown* (Rotterdam, 1999); a special issue of *El Croquis* (no. 86) was devoted to MVRDV in 1997.

NEUTELINGS RIEDIJK

Willem Jan Neutelings (born Bergen op Zoom, 1959) graduated from the Delft University of Technology in 1986. After working for OMA from 1981 to 1986, he established architectural practices in Amsterdam and Rotterdam. In 1997 he entered into a partnership with Michiel Riedijk (born Geldrop, 1964), who graduated from Delft University in 1989. Neutelings has been a guest lecturer at the Berlage Institute in Amsterdam and a visiting professor at the Graduate School of Design of Harvard University in Boston. Riedijk has been a lecturer at Delft University of Technology and at the Academy of Architecture in Amsterdam. The firm's most important completed projects include the Minnaert Building at the University of Utrecht (1997), Veenman Printers in Ede (1997), Steunpunt Rijkswaterstaat in Haarlingen (1998) and fire stations in Breda and Maastricht (1999). Publications about the firm include *Willem Jan Neutelings Architect* (Rotterdam, 1991) and a special issue of *El Croquis* (no. 94, 1999).

NOX

NOX is headed by Lars Spuybroek (born Rotterdam, 1959), who graduated from Delft University of Technology in 1989. He has lectured at Delft University of Technology, the Berlage Institute in Amsterdam, the Eindhoven University of Technology and Columbia University in New York. NOX's completed projects include a conversion for the video production studio VBC in Amsteram (1992), the H_2O eXPO Pavilion (Neeltje Jans, 1994–97) and the V2 Media Lab in Rotterdam (1998). Publications by NOX include *NOX A Actiones in Distans* (Amsterdam, 1991; with Maurice Nio), *NOX B Biotech* (Amsterdam, 1992; with Maurice Nio), *NOX C Chloroform* (Amsterdam, 1993; with Maurice Nio), *Nox D Djihad* (Amsterdam, 1994; with Maurice Nio), *The Art of the Accident* (Rotterdam, 1998; ed. with Joke Brouwer) and *Deep Surface* (Rotterdam, 1999). Lars Spuybroek was the editor of *Forum* from 1994 to 1997 and guest editor of the January 2000 issue of *Domus* (no. 822).

OFFICE OF METROPOLITAN ARCHITECTURE (OMA)

After working as a journalist for *De Haagse Post* and a scenarist, Rem Koolhaas (born Rotterdam, 1944) went to study at the Architectural Association in London from 1968 to 1972 and Cornell University in Ithaca, New York, from 1972 to 1973. He was a visiting fellow at the Institute for Architecture and Urbanism (IAUS) in New York from 1973 to 1979. In 1975 Koolhaas founded the Office for Metropolitan Architecture (OMA) in London with Elia and Zoe Zenghelis and Madelon Vriesendorp. A branch opened in Rotterdam in 1978 and has since expanded to become the head office. Koolhaas has taught at the Architectural Association in London, the University of California at Los Angeles, the Institute for Urban Studies in New York, Delft University of Technology, Harvard University in Boston, Rice University in Houston and the Berlage Institute in Amsterdam. The firm's most important competed projects include the Nederlands Dans Theater in The Hague (1987), the NEXUS housing project in Fukuoka (1991), the Villa dall'Ava in Paris (1991), the KunstHAL in Rotterdam (1992), the master plan and the Congrexpo for Euralille (Lille, France, 1994), the Educatorium for the Univeristy of Utrecht (1997) and the Villa Bordeaux (1998). Koolhaas's own publications include *Delirious New York: A Retro-active Manifesto for Manhattan* (New York, London, Paris, 1978) and *S, M, L, XL* (Rotterdam, New York, 1995; with Bruce Mau). Among the special magazine issues devoted to OMA and Rem Koolhaas have been two issues of *El Croquis* (nos 53 and 79).

OOSTERHUIS.NL

Kas Oosterhuis (born Amersfoort, 1951) graduated from the Delft University of Technology in 1979. He has lectured at the Architectural Association in London and been a professor at Delft University of Technology since 2000. He established Kas Oosterhuis Architekten in Rotterdam in 1988, which, with his partner Ilona Lénárd, is known today as Oosterhuisassociates. The firm's most important built works are the saltwaterpavilion (Neeltje Jans, 1997) and paraSITE (Rotterdam, Helsinki, Dunaújváros, Graz, The Hague, 1997–98). Oosterhuis has published several books, including *City Fruitful* (Rotterdam, 1992), *Sculpture City* (Rotterdam, 1995), *Kas Oosterhuis Architect, Ilona Lénárd Visual Artist* (Rotterdam, 1998) and *Writings 1990–2000* (Rotterdam, 2000).

KOEN VAN VELSEN

Before graduating from the Academy of Architecture in Amsterdam in 1983, Koen van Velsen (born Hilversum, 1952) had already started his own firm in Hilversum in 1977. His most important works are Discothèque Slinger (Hilversum, 1978–79), the van Velsen shop and house (Hilversum, 1980–81), alterations to the Armamentarium (Delft, 1982–89), alteration of the Ministry of Welfare, Public Health and Culture building (Rijswijk, 1985–86), a public library in Zeewolde (1985–89), Rijksakademie van Beeldende Kunsten (Amsterdam, 1985–92), alteration of Hotel Gooiland (Hilversum, 1989–90), Megacinama multiplex theatre (Rotterdam, 1992–96), the Town Hall in Terneuzen (1994–97) and the Film Academy in Amsterdam (1995–99). Janny Rodermond has written a monograph, *Koen van Velsen, Architect* (Rotterdam, 1995).

WEST 8/ADRIAAN GEUZE

Upon completing a degree in landscape architecture at the University of Wageningen in 1987, Adriaan Geuze (born Dordrecht, 1960) founded West 8 Landscape Architects in Rotterdam with Paul van Beek, who has since left the firm. West 8 is active in all aspects of landscape design, from such large-scale projects as the landscaping of Schiphol airport (1991–) and the transformation of an agricultural area in the province of Groningen into a recreation zone (1995). Other projects include urban designs for Borneo and Sporenburg districts in Amsterdam (1994–present) and for the Vathorst district of Amersfoort (1996–present), public squares such as Schouwburgplein (1991–96) and Binnenrotte (1991–95) in Rotterdam, the Carrascoplein park in Amsterdam (1992–97) and the Central Park in Leidsche Rijn (1997–present) and gardens like those for Centrum Beeldende Kunst in Dordrecht (1993–95), Verenigde Spaarbank in Utrecht (1993–95) and Interpolis in Tilburg (1995–97). Adriaan Geuze has lectured at the École Nationale Supérieure de Paysage in Versailles, the Berlage Institute in Amsterdam and Harvard University in Boston, and has been a professor at the Delft University of Technology. Publications by Adriaan Geuze and West 8 include *In Holland staat een huis* (Rotterdam, 1995), *Colonizing the Void* (Rotterdam/Venice, 1996), *Adriaan Geuze/West 8 Landscape Architects* (eds Bart Lootsma and Inge Breugem, Rotterdam, 1996) and *90,000 pakjes margarine, 100 meter vooruit, West 8 over landschap in acceleratie* (Groningen, 1997).

WIEL ARETS

AZL Pensionfund Building, Heerlen
Architect: Wiel Arets; project architects: Dominic Papa, Jo Janssen, Ani Velez; collaborators: Malin Johanson, Maurice Paulussen, Joanna Tang, René Thijssen, Hein Urlings, Richard Welten

Academy of Arts and Architecture, Maastricht
Architect: Wiel Arets; project architect: Jo Janssen; collaborators: René Holten, Anita Morandini, Maurice Paulussen, Richard Welten

Police Station, Vaals
Architect: Wiel Arets; project architect: Rhea Harbers; collaborators: Delphine Clavien, Paul Egers, Michel Melenhorst

Police Station, Cuijck
Architect: Wiel Arets; project architects: Ralph van Mameren, René Thijssen; site engineer: Hein Urlings, project staff: Paul van Dongen, Harold Hermans, Dorte Jensen, Michel Melenhorst

UN STUDIO (VAN BERKEL & BOS)

Karbouw Building, Amersfoort
Architect: Ben van Berkel; collaborators: Aad Krom (project coordination), Kasper Aussems

REMU 50/10 kV Distribution Substation, Amersfoort
Architect: Ben van Berkel; project team: Harrie Pappot (project coordination), Pieter Koster, Hugo Beschoor Plug, Jaap Punt, John Rebel

Erasmus Bridge, Rotterdam
Architect: Ben van Berkel; collaborators: Freek Loos (project coordination), Hans Cromjongh, Ger Gijzen, Willemijn Lofvers, Sibo de Man, Gerard Nijenhuis, Manon Patinama, John Rebel, Ernst van Rijn, Hugo Schuurman, Caspar Smeets, Paul Toornend, Jan Willem Walraad, Dick Wetzels, Karel Vollers

Möbius House
Architect: Ben van Berkel; collaborators: Aad Krom (project coordination), Jen Alkema, Casper le Fèbre, Bob Hootsmans, Matthias Blass, Marc Dijkman, Remco Bruggink, Tycho Soffree, Harm Wassink, G. Tedesco, interior design: Ben van Berkel, Hans Knyvenhoven, Jen Alkema, Matthias Blass

ERICK VAN EGERAAT

ING/Nationale Nederlanden Building, Budapest
Design team: Erick van Egeraat, Tibor Gáll, Attila Komjáthy, Maartje Lammers, Astrid Huwald, Gábor Kruppa, János Tiba, Stephen Moylan, William Richards, Dianne Anyika, Paul-Martin Lied, Emmett Scanlon, Ineke Dubbeldam, Ard Buijsen, Miranda Nieboer, Harry Boxelaar, Axel Koschany, Tamara Klassen

Nature Museum, Rotterdam
Design team: Erick van Egeraat, Francine Houben, Birgit Jürgenhake, Perry Klootwijk, Jeroen Schipper, Jan Bekkering, Dietmar Haupt, Theo Kupers, Alexandre Lamboley, Miranda Nieboer, Luis Pires

Technical High School, Utrecht
Design team: Erick van Egeraat, Maartje Lammers, Ard Buijsen, Boris Zeisser

MECANOO

Faculty of Economics and Management Building, Utrecht
Project architects: Erick van Egeraat, Francine Houben, Chris de Weijer; collaborating architect: Henk Döll; assistant architect: Monica Adams; project manager: Aart Fransen; project staff: Carlo Bevers, Giuseppina Borri, Birgit de Bruin, Ard Buijsen, Harry Kurzhals, Miranda Nieboer, William Richards, Mechthild Stuhlmacher, Nathalie de Vries, Wim van Zijl; landscape architects: Marjolijn Adriaansche, Katja van Dalen, Annemieke Diekman; model: Henk Bouwer; supervising engineer: Gerrit Bras

Houber House and Studio, Rotterdam
Design team: Erick van Egeraat, Francine Houben

Library, University of Technology, Delft
Project architects: Francine Houben, Chris de Weijer; collaborating architect: Erik van Egeraat; project manager: Aart Fransen; project staff: Carlo Bevers, Monica Adams, Marjolijn Adriaansche, Jan Bekkering, Birgit de Bruin, Ard Bruijsen, Katja van Dalen, Annemieke Diekman, Ineke Dubbeldam, Alfa Hügelmann, Axel Koschany, Theo Kupers, Maartje Lammers, Paul Martin Lied, Bas Streppel, Astrid van Vliet, Gerrit Bras

MVRDV

VPRO Building, Hilversum
Design: Winy Maas, Jacob van Rijs and Nathalie de Vries, with Stefan Witteman, Alex Brouwer, Joost Glissenaar, Arjan Mulder, Eline Strijkers, Willem Timmer, Jaap van Dijk, Fokke Moerel, Joost Kok; facilitary office: Bureau Bouwkunde, Rotterdam

Villa KBWW, Utrecht
Design: De Architectengroep loerakker rijnboutt ruijssenaars hendriks van gameren mastenbroek bv – Bjarne Mastenbroek, with Floor Arons and Michiel Raaphorst and MVRDV – Winy Maas, Jacob van Rijs and Nathalie de Vries, with Mike Booth, Joost Glissenaar

WoZoCo's, Amsterdam
Design: Winy Maas, Jacob van Rijs and Nathalie de Vries, with Willem Timmer, Arjan Mulder, Frans de Witte; facilitary office: Bureau Bouwkunde, Rotterdam

Metacity/Datatown
Based on a video installation of the same title produced by MVRDV for the Stroom Centre of Visual Arts, The Hague, and exhibited from 12 December 1998 to 13 February 1999. The video installation was the second part of the project 'Metacity', which was conceived by Jan van Grunsven, Winy Maas and Arno van der Mark in collaboration with Stroom. Research and production were executed by MVRDV: Winy Maas, Jacob van Rijs and Nathalie de Vries, with Bas van Neijenhof, Mathurin Hardel, Ximo Peris Casado, Margarita Salmeron Espinosa, Eline Wieland, Marino Gouwens, Ali Rahim, Kok Kian Goh, Penelope Dean, Christoph Schindler, Nicole Meijer, Paul Ouwerkerk and Joost Grootens. The installation was made possible by the financial support of the Stimuleringsfonds voor Architectuur, Fonds voor Beeldende Kunsten, Vormgeving en Bouwkunst en Stroom

Dutch Pavilion for Expo 2000, Hanover
Design: Winy Maas, Jacob van Rijs and Nathalie de Vries, with Stefan Witteman, Jaap van Dijk, Christoph Schindler, Kristina Adsersen, Rüdiger Kreiselmayer; concept phase: Winy Maas, Jacob van Rijs and Nathalie de Vries, with Philipp Oswalt, Joost Grootens, Christelle Gualdi, Eline Strijkers, Martin Young; visualization: GroupA; model: Vincent de Rijk

NEUTELINGS RIEDIJK

Minnaert Building, Utrecht
Design team: Willem Jan Neutelings, Michiel Riedijk, Jonathan Woodroffe, Evert Crols, Jago van Bergen, Gerrit Schilder, Burton Hamfelt, Chidi Onwuka, Joost Mulders

Veenman Printers, Ede
Design Team: Willem Jan Neutelings, Michiel Riedijk, Willem Bruijn, Dirk van den Heuvel, Andy Woodcock

Post Office, Scherpenheuvel, Belgium
Design team: Willem Jan Neutelings, Michiel Riedijk, Bart Biermans, Andy Woodcock

Fire Station, Maastricht
Design team: Willem Jan Neutelings, Michiel Riedijk, Jago van Bergen, Juliette Bekkering, Bas Suijkerbuijk, Hilda Cohen

NOX
H$_2$O eXPO Pavilion, Neeltje Jans
Design: NOX/Lars Spuybroek; project team: Joan Almekinders, Maurice Nio, Pieter Heymans, William Veerbeek; interactive design installations: Lars Spuybroek; composer: Victor Wentinck; sensor development: Bert Bongers; lighting: euroGenie, Laurens van Manen, Mathijs van Manen (hardware), Floris van Manen (software); projections: Instituut Calibre, Walther Roelen (ripples), Jo Mantelers (wave), Daniel Dekkers (blob)
V2 Lab, Rotterdam
Design: NOX/Lars Spuybroek, with Joan Almekinders, Pieter Heymans
D-tower
Mediatower for the city of Doetinchem, collaboration with Rotterdam-based artist Q.S. Serafijn
Off-the-Road 5-speed
Non-standard prefabricated housing near highway A58, Eindhoven
Client: TRUDO housing corporation
Design: NOX/Lars Spuybroek, with Joan Almekinders and Joke Brouwer

OFFICE OF METROPOLITAN ARCHITECTURE (OMA)
KunstHAL, Rotterdam
Design: Rem Koolhaas, Fuminori Hoshino; team: Toni Adam, Isaac Batenburg, Leo van Immerzeel, Herman Jacobs, Jo Schippers, Ron Steiner
Library, Jussieu (Paris)
Competition design: Rem Koolhaas, Christophe Cornubert, Xaveer de Geyter, René Heijne, Markus Röthlisberger, Yushi Uehara with Hernando Arrazola, Siebe Bakker, Gary Bates, Gro Bonesmo, Arjen de Groot, Jerry Kopare, Markus Lüscher, Peter Oudshoorn, Jacob van Rijs, Roland Stuy; preliminary design: Rem Koolhaas, Christophe Cornubert, Anne Mie Depuydt, René Heijne, Winy Maas, Jacob van Rijs with Matthias Bauer, Frans Blok, Patrick Cosmao, Michael Hsu, Ray Maggiore; engineers: Ove Arup & Partners – Cecil Balmond (structural), Rory McGowan (structural), Crispin Matson (mechanical), Sean Billings (façade), Coyne Bellier; program consultants: DA & DU; adviser: Jean Attali; model: Daan Bakker, René Heijne, Ad Kliphuis, Markus Lüscher, Gijs Niemeyer, Stein Vossen, Ronald Wall
Educatorium, Utrecht
Project architects: Rem Koolhaas, Christophe Cornubert; preliminary design: Rem Koolhaas, Christophe Cornubert, Gary Bates, Luc Veeger, Clement Gillet; team: Richard Eelman, Michel Melenhorst,

Jacques Vink, Gaudi Houdaya, Enno Sternerding, Frans Blok, Henrik Valeur, Boukje Trenning
Masterplan and Congrexpo, Lille
Design: Rem Koolhaas/OMA; associate architects: François Delhay; preliminary design workshop: Rem Koolhaas, Floris Alkemade, Douglas Grieco, Jan-Willem van Kuilenburg, Ray Maggiore, Eduardo Arroyo Munoz, Jim Njoo, Mark Schendel, Yushi Uehara, Sarah Whiting, William Wilson; design development: (OMA) Rem Koolhaas, with Rients Dijkstra, Jan-Willem van Kuilenburg, Ray Maggiore, Mark Schendel, Yushi Uehara, Ron Witte, Dirk Zuiderveld (FM Delhay) François Delhay, François Brevart, Christophe d'Hulst; final design: (OMA) Rem Koolhaas, with Ruud Cobussen, Jan-Willem van Kuilenburg, Ray Maggiore, Mark Schendel, Diana Stiles, Luc Veeger, Ron Witte; (FM Delhay): François Delhay, François Brevart, Christophe d'Hulst, Shoreh Davar Panah, Isabelle Lemetay, James Lenglin, Olivier Tourraine; construction (OMA) Rem Koolhaas, Mark Schendel, with Ruud Cobussen, Jeanne Gang, Diana Stiles; (FM Delhay): François Delhay, François Brevart, with Xavier d'Alençon, Christophe d'Hulst, Bertrand Fages; interior finishings, furniture: Petra Blaisse in collaboration with Julie Sfez; textiles (auditorium curtains, Expo linen screen): Petra Blaisse; structural engineers: Ove Arup & Partners – Cecil Balmond, Rory McGowan, Robert Pugh, Mohsen Zikri (mechanical); services engineers: Joel Taquet, Pascal Beckaert, Gérard Cattuti, Bruno Fontana, Bruno Loiseleux, Sodeg; façade consultant: Robert-Jan van Santen, Agence van Stanten; scenography: Agence Ducks, Michel Cova; acoustics: Rens van Luxemburg, TNO; quantity surveyor: Bernard Gaillet, Jean-Marie Nuclain, Cabinet Gaillet; bureau de contrôle: Christiaan Theys, Socotec; planning: Mr Talpin, Jean Foerderer, GEMO; synthèse: SETIB, Yves de Ponthrud; general contractor: Dumez-Quillery SNEP
Villa Bordeaux
Conception: OMA/Rem Koolhaas, with Jeanne Gang, Julien Monfort, Jeroen Thomas, Bill Price and Yo Yamagata, Chris Dondorp, Vincent Costes, Erik Schotte; codesigner for platform with security devices, fixed furniture, kitchen, library and master bedroom bathroom: MVS – Maarten van Severen and Raf De Preter; executive architect: Regaud Ingenierie; Michel Regaud; structural engineer; Ove Arup & Partners – Cecil Balmond and Robert Pugh; façade development: Van

Santen – Robert-Jan van Santen; hydraulics development for platform: A.T.H. – Gerard Couillandeau; advice interiors: Inside/Outside – Petra Blaisse
Public toilet, Groningen
Design: Rem Koolhaas, Gro Bonesmo, i.c.w. Erwin Olaf

OOSTERHUIS.NL
Garbage Transfer Station, Zenderen
Design team: Kas Oosterhuis, architect; Ilona Lénárd, visual artist; Leo Donkersloot, visual artist; Niek van Vliet, architect
H$_2$O eXPO Pavilion, Neeltje Jans
Project architect: Kas Oosterhuis, Menno Rubbens, Ilona Lénárd; project staff: Adrian Fisher, Marjo Kekkonen, Marino Gouwens, Eline Wieland, Károly Tóth
ParaSITE, Rotterdam
Design: Ilona Lénárd, visual artist; Kas Oosterhuis, architect; parascape language composer: Richard Tolenaar and Johan van der Kreij

KOEN VAN VELSEN
Megacinema, Rotterdam
Project staff: Lars Zwart, Gero Rutten, Marcel Steeghs, Okko van der Kam
Town Hall, Terneuzen
project staff: Gideon de Jong, Okko van der Kam, Lars Zwart, Marcel Steeghs
Rijksakademie, Amsterdam
Design team: Koen van Velsen, Geert de Boer, Maarten van der Hulst, Timo Keulen, Gero Rutten, Lars Zwart

WEST 8/ADRIAAN GEUZE
Borneo and Sporenburg Urban Designs, Amsterdam
Design team: Adriaan Geuze, Wim Kloosterboer, Yushi Uehara, Sebastiaan Riquois
Schouwburgplein, Rotterdam
Design team: Adraan Geuze, Wim Kloosterboer, Dirry de Bruin, Cyrus B Clark, Erwin Bot, Dick Heydra, Huub Juurlink, Nigel Sampey, Erik Overdiep, Jurgen Beij, Jerry van Eyck
Interpolis Gardens, Tilburg
Design team: Adriaan Geuze, Cyrus B Clark, David Buurma, Edwin van der Hoeven, Erik Overdiep, Guido Marsille, Jan Paul de Ridder, Sibil Sträuli
Carrascoplein, Amsterdam
Design team: Adriaan Geuze, Inge Breugem, Dirry de Bruin, Katrien Prak, Olivier Scheffer, Huub Juurlink, Erwin Bot, Jörg Schiemann
Oosterschelde Flood Barrier
Design team: Adriaan Geuze, Paul van Beek, Dirry de Bruin, Huub Juurlink, Erik Overdiep